GRAFANA BANANA: DASHBOARDS, DRAMA & DATA DISASTERS

ABOUT THE AUTHOR

With decades of experience spanning various domains of IT—including project management, development, database administration, and marketing—this author has cultivated a unique perspective that blends technical know-how with strategic insight. Their depth of expertise lends credibility to their work, resulting in a compelling voice that resonates throughout Grafana Banana: Dashboards, Drama & Data Disasters. The author's extensive background allows them to navigate the complexities of the tech world, making them a trusted guide for both novices and experienced professionals alike.

Having worked in diverse roles across multiple sectors, the author brings a wealth of practical experience to the table. From steering projects to successful completions to managing intricate data systems, they have encountered and overcome numerous challenges. This hands-on experience forms the backbone of their narrative, illustrating real-world applications of the concepts discussed in their book. By sharing stories of data disasters and triumphs, the author effectively bridges the gap between theory and practice, providing readers with relatable scenarios that enhance learning.

The author holds several prestigious qualifications within the IT field, which serve to enrich their writing and impart valuable knowledge. Their writing journey began as a means to document lessons learned and solutions found in the face of adversity. This passion for storytelling coupled with a desire to educate has culminated in the creation of Grafana Banana. The author is not just a practitioner; they are an advocate for leveraging data as a powerful tool for decision-making and innovation.

When not immersed in the intricacies of IT, the author enjoys connecting with readers through their engaging writing style, characterized by a blend of humor, relatability, and clarity. Their approach is not merely to inform but also to inspire action and provoke thought. Readers will find an accessible narrative that demystifies complex topics, encouraging them to take bold steps in their own data journeys. The author believes that effective communication, regardless of the audience, is key to success in the ever-evolving tech landscape.

Ultimately, the author's mission is to enlighten, empower, and enable professionals to harness the power of data in meaningful ways. With a commitment to sharing knowledge and fostering an environment of continuous learning, they plan to write more books that tackle pressing issues in technology and project management. As they look to the future, they aspire to conduct workshops and speaking engagements that will further elevate their mission to transform the way we think about and work with data.

TABLE OF CONTENTS

CHAPTER 1 – THE CULT OF THE DASHBOARD

CHAPTER 2 – THE GRAFANA GOBLIN ATE MY QUERIES

CHAPTER 3 – IT'S NOT A BUG, IT'S A PANEL FEATURE

CHAPTER 4 – QUERY LIKE NOBODY'S WATCHING

CHAPTER 5 – ALERT! ALERT! PANIC NOT REQUIRED

CHAPTER 6 – USERS, ROLES, AND THE ART OF CONTROLLED CHAOS

CHAPTER 7 – PLUGIN ROULETTE AND OTHER DANGEROUS GAMES

CHAPTER 8 – A BACKUP WALKS INTO A BAR...

CHAPTER 9 – HIGH AVAILABILITY OR HIGH ANXIETY?

CHAPTER 10 – THE DASHBOARD GRAVEYARD

CHAPTER 11 –
TEMPLATING AND
OTHER BLACK MAGIC

CHAPTER 12 – MONITORING THE MONITOR

CHAPTER 13 – GRAFANA VS. THE END USERS

(1) - 13.1 The User Experience: Understanding Dashboard Interaction

(2) - 13.2 The 'Click Everything' Phenomenon: A Case Study

(3) - 13.3 Child-Proofing Your Dashboard: Strategies for User Safety

CHAPTER 14 – GRAFANA CLOUD, ENTERPRISE, OR THE BASEMENT BEAST YOU MAINTAIN ALONE

CHAPTER 15 – ZEN AND THE ART OF DASHBOARD MAINTENANCE

APPENDIX A: THE GRAFANA CLI COOKBOOK

APPENDIX B: 101 EXCUSES FOR WHEN ALERTS GO OFF AT 3AM

(1) - B.1 The Best (and Worst) Excuses to Tell Your Boss

(2) - B.2 Avoiding the 'Oops' Moment: How to Prepare

(3) - B.3 Turning Chaos into Humor: Making Light of Late Night Alerts

APPENDIX C:
DASHBOARD HAIKU
AND ASCII ART

CHAPTER 1 – THE CULT OF THE DASHBOARD

1.1 The Holy Grail Of Visualizations: An Introduction To Grafana

Imagine a realm where your data doesn't just sit there, gathering digital dust. Instead, it becomes a vibrant tapestry of colors and shapes, a visual feast that could make even abstract artists envious. Grafana is that magical place where graphs aren't just lines on a boring spreadsheet; they're dynamic displays of insight, each curve telling tales that could rival any soap opera. The sheer excitement of slinging dashboards together, like a mad scientist in a lab of data, is intoxicating. You'll find yourself giggling with glee as you watch those numbers transform into visual narratives, bringing your analyses to life in ways you never thought possible. It's almost like your data is throwing a party, and you're the DJ, spinning tracks of information that groove right into the hearts of your viewers.

In this wacky adventure through charts and panels, you'll discover that leaving your data trapped in a CSV file is like keeping a lion in a cardboard box; it's just not fair to anyone involved. Grafana provides the tools to unleash your data's wild side, allowing you to create visualizations that captivate, engage, and yes, even dazzle. With interactive features and an array of plugins, you can turn mundane metrics into mesmerizing masterpieces. Suddenly, time series data transforms into a thrilling ride through the past, present, and future, allowing even the most hesitant stakeholders to join your data journey. Remember, every time you build a new dashboard, you're not just arranging numbers; you're weaving a story that invites everyone to witness the magic of data-driven decisions. So grab your virtual paintbrush and get ready to make pixels dance!

1.2 Installing Grafana On Carl: A Love Story

To win over Carl, your loyal server companion, the first step is to set the mood. A little jazz in the background can make the installation process feel less like a daunting task and more like a romantic comedy. Start by ensuring Carl has all the prerequisites —some cozy dependencies ready to embrace Grafana. Make sure your package manager is up to date, which is sort of like checking Carl's pulse. This is essential before diving into the actual installation.

Now, when you're ready to serenade Carl with some command-line commands, don't forget to use your best charm. Fetch the latest version of Grafana like it's a bouquet of roses; this is the gift you're offering Carl. Use commands that would make any tech stack swoon. As you quietly invoke the installation command, imagine Carl blushing under all those circuits and cables— configure paths, set up service files, and maybe even sprinkle some touch commands for good measure. Personal touches are paramount in this love story.

Every love story has its ups and downs, and as you coax Carl to host Grafana, you might find yourself facing challenges that make you want to channel your inner puppy dog. Perhaps you encounter misconfigured permissions or a firewall that seems determined to thwart your romantic endeavors. At this point, throwing a well-timed emotive sigh may help, as though asking, "Why, Carl, why?" With determination and a good bit of googling, you can navigate these hurdles. Rethink settings, open ports, on occasion, even make that heartfelt appeal to the error logs, gently pleading for guidance.

Remember, persistence is key in both love and server management. As you adjust configurations to allow Grafana to flourish under Carl's roof, you'll find that every struggle only enhances the love story. Each solved error is like a small victory shared between you two, building a stronger bond. Eventually, when Grafana springs to life on Carl, a sense of triumph lights up the room and you feel like a tech-savvy cupid. Embrace the journey and don't shy away from using a little humor—nothing says love quite like the playful banter of installation script errors.

As you wrap this delightful installation process, always remember that patience and creativity are your greatest allies when courting technology. Even when Carl throws a tantrum, approach it with a wink and a grin, because every sweet setup leads to beautifully crafted dashboards filled with data-driven love.

1.3 The First 37 Slack Notifications: Welcome To Monitoring Madness

The moment you set up your real-time monitoring, a wave of excitement washes over you. You're now the proud owner of a constant stream of insights, alerts, and, let's be honest, utter chaos as your Slack channels explode with notifications. It's like hosting a party where you invited every data point, and they're all crashing the door at once. With each refreshing panel that displays a new metric, your heart races, mirroring the rise and fall of your server's CPU usage. You begin to wonder if you've accidentally signed up for an unlimited subscription to stress because those 37 notifications in five minutes? Yes, they're definitely a *thing*. Suddenly, Slack sounds less like a communication tool and more like a raucous sports event where every twist and turn could mean glory or doom.

While it's thrilling to keep tabs on your server and see it perform like a well-oiled machine, it's essential to manage the impending notification overload. Having a hundred incoming alerts might feel cathartic at first but can quickly morph into a dizzying fiasco that would make even the calmest of souls twitch. Start by silencing notifications for non-essential alerts that feel like your coworkers yelling from across the office; if the server occasionally hiccups, it doesn't mean we need an all-out state of emergency. Set your primary focus on those critical alerts that signal real trouble—like when the CPU temperature hits "I'm melting!" levels. You could even rotisserie chicken in the data flames before the team realizes what's at stake. Ultimately, learning to differentiate between minor glitches and server catastrophes will save your sanity and your job. Also, schedule dedicated 'alert review' times to sort through the chaos and reduce constant distractions. Just remember: your Slack should enhance your workflow, not give you an anxiety-induced caffeine high.

CHAPTER 2 – THE GRAFANA GOBLIN ATE MY QUERIES

2.1 Integrating Data Sources: The Good, The Bad, And The Goblin

Integrating data sources can feel like hosting a party where all your guests have different tastes in music. You want them to enjoy their time together, but instead, they're fighting over who gets to choose the playlist. Fortunately, when you successfully integrate data sources, it's like finding the ultimate DJ that magically synchronizes everything, and everyone is dancing in unison. Picture this: your databases, APIs, and server logs all blissfully jamming together, creating a symphony of insights. With a good integration strategy, data flows from various sources seamlessly, giving you a grand overview of your metrics while your analytics dashboard serves as the spotlights illuminating your marvelous data dance floor. And fear not, because with the right tools and techniques, you can wave goodbye to pesky goblins that might otherwise derail the festivities. These little troublemakers often embody poorly defined data formats, inconsistent schemas, or those pesky plugins that don't quite play nice, turning your integration party into a chaotic free-for-all. Thus, implementing a unified strategy, like creating a data dictionary or utilizing ETL processes, is essential. It promotes harmony within the disparate elements of your data sources, allowing for a smoother integration experience without the goblins tripping over the cords.

However, the road to seamless data integration is not paved with marshmallows and rainbows. Oh no! It can be littered with pitfalls that can send your project spiraling into chaos faster than a toddler throwing a tantrum over a dropped ice cream cone. One of the prime suspects in this debacle is data redundancy, where the same data exists in multiple locations and each version tells a different story. This is like asking your friends to suggest a movie, and everyone throws out their recommendations without checking what the others have said, resulting in a night of utter confusion. Then there's the data quality issue, where old or stale data refuses to cooperate, leading to inaccurate reports that make you question whether you should pursue a career in interpretive dance instead. Furthermore, if you're relying on a mishmash of old database systems that don't communicate well, you may find yourself in a constant state of 'data whispering,' trying to interpret the secrets each source refuses to share directly. You also have to deal with the dreaded API limits – those constraints that feel like you're trying to squeeze a giant inflatable dinosaur into a tiny doorframe. Bumping into these pitfalls can lead to anger-inducing outcomes that could make you want to throw your laptop out the window. Remember, a thorough design and planning phase, along with regular audits of your data sources, can help you avoid these melodramatic scenarios. Keep your integration smooth by addressing these issues before they become the goblins at your data party.

Make sure to incorporate regular assessments of your integration process, scrutinizing both your data quality and the flow of information. Think of it as maintaining a well-tended garden – remove the weeds and nurture the flowers to ensure a vibrant and fruitful outcome.

2.2 Plugin Overload: Choosing The Right Add-Ons

Navigating the chaotic jungle of plugins can feel like wandering through a wild amusement park, except every ride is labeled with enticing promises and hidden risks. Each plugin you encounter seems like a friendly new friend, beaming at you from the shadows, whispering sweet nothings about features that will revolutionize your Grafana experience. However, proceed with caution! Not every add-on will be your ally; some come with layers of complexity that'll make your head spin faster than a tilt-a-whirl on a bad day. It's like choosing the right toppings for a pizza—too many, and you end up with a messy slice that's impossible to hold. With great power comes great responsibility, or in this case, a trip to the error log when a plugin crashes like a clown off a seesaw. So, grab your digital machete and cut through the underbrush of flashy icons and promises. Choose your add-ons wisely, or you might wake up one day surrounded by the ghostly remnants of unused plugins and a dashboard that resembles a chaotic art project.

Uncovering the must-have plugins while avoiding the dreaded 'what have I done?' moment is the name of the game, and luckily, this isn't a game of chance—though it often feels like roulette. You don't want to blindly slap on every shiny plugin that catches your eye. Instead, think of plugins as your loyal sidekicks in the noble quest for optimal performance. A good plugin helps you visualize data in dazzling ways, like casting a spell that turns numbers into glorious rainbows on screen. Must-haves in your toolkit include those that enhance data visualization, integrate different data sources smoothly, and alert you when things go wrong without turning every minor hiccup into a full-blown thunderstorm of notifications. Get to know your plugins like you'd get to know your quirky team members; learn what they excel at, how they mesh with the rest of your setup, and what pantry items they might accidentally spill all over the floor. By selecting the right combination, you can craft a dashboard that's not just functional, but also a delightful visual feast, minus the messy aftermath of an office potluck gone awry. So, approach with a plan, make informed choices, and save your sanity while securing your dashboard's longevity.

2.3 The Case Of The Half-Rendered Pie Chart: Debugging Disasters

Half-pie charts can be the spectral shadows lurking in the dark corners of your Grafana visuals, and spotting one can send chills down your spine. Imagine working tirelessly on a dashboard, meticulously feeding it data like a digital gardener tending to a fragile plant, only to be ambushed by a pie chart that looks like it was devoured by a hungry troll. You know the one: perfectly round on one half and shockingly absent on the other, like a pizza slice that got lost in transit. The issues behind this spectral phenomenon often stem from query mishaps, data mismatches, or, heaven forbid, an update that turned your pie to a quarter pie. The fear of the half-pie chart is not just a figment of your imagination; it's a very real consequence of data not flowing or rendering as it should, taunting you like a ghost with a penchant for chaos.

When faced with the vexing ghost of a half-rendered pie chart, don't panic! Instead, channel your inner debug ninja and unleash your powers. Begin by examining your data queries with the precision of a detective scrutinizing a crime scene; check if your data source is correctly set up and look for missing data that could be responsible for the chart's spectral state. A heart-pounding, nail-biting moment will envelop you as you make adjustments one at a time, wielding each change like a lightsaber in a galactic battle against the forces of bad data visualization. Don't forget to leverage Grafana's logging features, as they can often reveal the hidden culprits behind your chart's plight. When your pie finally renders in its full glory, you'll have a moment of sheer joy as you bask in the glow of a success story—high-fives all around! And remember, never underestimate the power of a well-placed refresh. Sometimes all it takes is a little patience—and a sprinkle of debugging magic—to transform your despair into a triumphant yay!

CHAPTER 3 – IT'S NOT A BUG, IT'S A PANEL FEATURE

3.1 Understanding Panels: Types And Uses

Diving deep into the colorful universe of panels can feel like taking a joyride through a candy store, where each panel type is a different sugary delight just waiting to be discovered. Panels in a dashboard are like the quirky characters in a circus—each has a unique personality and purpose to make your data display not just informative but a true visual extravaganza. From graphs that pulse like they're at a rave to status indicators that scream "I need help over here!", understanding panels means unlocking the potential to transform mundane data into delightful insights. Imagine a world where your time series data doesn't just sit there but dances in rhythmic harmony across a line chart, or a world where a pie chart isn't just a sad slice of confusion but becomes an enticing dessert plate spilling over with delicious details. Yes, my friends, the right panels can sprinkle magic over your dashboard, turning chaotic data into something as captivating as a Broadway show.

To further achieve your visual nirvana, one must identify specific panel types tailored to your data's personality. Are you trying to show trends over time? A line chart is your trusted steed. Do you have categorical data that needs to sparkle? Look no further than a bar chart that stands tall and proud. For the data that cries for context, a table can organize chaos into clean rows and columns, whispering "Look at me, I have structure!" And let's not forget the ever-popular single stat panel, echoing that lovingly reassuring message, "Yes, you are indeed on track." Understanding these various types allows you to harness the right panel for the right occasion, like swapping out a clown suit for a tuxedo when it's time to impress your boss or that special someone. Layer in time filters, and suddenly you can navigate back and forth through your data like a magician pulling rabbits from a hat. You can present historic trends alongside real-time data, making it seem as though your dashboard is not just showing the past or the present, but actually telling a story.

Lastly, as you explore the expansive universe of panels, here's a fun tip: always keep a notepad and a cup of coffee handy. When inspiration strikes, and you suddenly picture how a perfectly aligned bar chart will create harmony without sending your viewers into a dizzying spiral, you don't want to forget about it. Sketch out your ideas, play with combinations of panels, and don't shy away from experimenting. Grafana is your canvas, and each panel type is a brush; mix them, blend them, and above all, enjoy the wild and colorful ride that data visualization can offer. After all, the goal is not just to inform but to engage your audience and maybe even make them chuckle or gasp in surprise.

3.2 Variables And Time Filters: The Dynamic Duo Of Dashboards

Variables are the secret sauce that transforms bland data into a fully animated, sparkling piñata of insights. Imagine variables as your quirky, unpredictable friend who doesn't just show up with a birthday cake but also brings fireworks, a mariachi band, and a rollercoaster ride—all in the name of exploring your data. When it comes to dashboards, variables are like the little wizards that can reshape your views based on user input, filtering your data with the grace of a ballerina while maintaining a sense of spontaneity like a dog chasing after its own tail. Need to compare data across different regions? Slap a variable in there, and voila! You're no longer looking through a foggy windshield but driving a convertible down the open highway of dashboards, hair blowing in the wind as insights come rushing at you.

Variables help you engage with your data dynamically. They allow you to play 'choose your own adventure'—where you're not just stuck reading page 12 but can effortlessly flip to the chapter that makes the most sense for your analysis at the moment. It's the difference between watching a flat, lifeless movie and being handed the special remote with variable buttons. Press one, and suddenly the plot twists, characters change, and you're seeing just how those sales figures in Seattle hold up against their SoCal rivals! If you keep variables fresh and fun, they can make users not only knowledgeable but absolutely jazzed about the insights they're creating.

Time filters are like the magical time-turner from Harry Potter, but instead of looking at missed classes, you can rewind and fast-forward through your historical data. Imagine waking up one morning and deciding you want to check sales data from last Tuesday instead of yesterday. With time filters, you can reach into the cosmic ether of your data and pull out just what you need, as though your dashboard were a mystical oracle that serves you tailored insights on demand. Want to see how a marketing campaign affected sales week by week? Just set the time filter, adjust your timeline like a seasoned DJ mixing beats, and you're set!

These filters can turn your big, static visuals into vibrant maps of historical trends and insights. You're not just looking at a snapshot in time; you're diving into a narrative that unfolds as you step through the moments. Plus, when you realize you can zoom in and out, just like pinching and expanding on your phone, it's game-over for static views that once ruled your world.

Mastering time filters means embracing the flow of data over time, adding a sensational flair that encourages users to become data explorers rather than mere spectators.

To keep your dashboard dynamically engaging, think about combining variables with time filters. Allow users to customize their view effectively while slicing through historical data, making each interaction a step into the wonderful world of insights. The more control you give your users, the more they will cherish the journey through your data!

3.3 When Line Charts Go Rogue: The Ekg Incident

The anatomy of line charts might seem straightforward, but before you know it, they can start giving off the vibes of a caffeinated goat on a sugar rush. A line chart typically comprises a series of points connected by straight lines, each representing data over a given period. Easy, right? Yet, like a goat that has just discovered espresso, these charts can take an unpredictable turn. You may find that what should be a smooth, steady line morphs into a jagged mess that resembles an EKG of a hyperactive creature. This can happen due to data anomalies—outliers that throw everything off course faster than a goat chasing after a carrot. A spike in user activity, a sudden server crash, or that mysterious data source that nobody dares to touch can create these twists and turns, resulting in a visualization that leaves you both puzzled and amused.

Once you find yourself staring at a rogue line chart, it's time to troubleshoot your way back to sanity and clarity. Begin this journey by questioning the sources of your data. Are there any unexpected values lurking beneath the surface? Did someone mix up the time zones like you're prepping for a convoluted scavenger hunt? Look closely at the trends—is this jagged line genuinely reflecting user behavior, or is it a prank pulled by mischievous server elves? Adjust your data range and visually inspect it for anomalies that could serve up unwelcome surprises in your charts. If necessary, plot your data points separately to identify the troublemakers before they run amok, thus restoring order to your visualizations.

One key takeaway is to validate your data before donning your chart wizard hat. By ensuring that your data pipeline is robust enough to handle the quirky personalities of your data points, you minimize the chance of being surprised by line charts that act like overtired goats. Regularly review your data inputs and outputs. It can save you the headache of diving into a tangled mess of erratic lines that can turn a simple data analysis task into an unexpected circus performance.

CHAPTER 4 – QUERY LIKE NOBODY'S WATCHING

4.1 The Language Of Data: Sql And Its Friends

When it comes to data querying, SQL stands tall like a superhero in a world of mere mortals, effortlessly flexing its muscles while other languages scuttle about like frightened little mice. Structured Query Language, or SQL, for those who haven't yet joined the cult of the dashboard, is the golden ticket to understanding and managing your databases. It's the language that makes even the simplest queries feel like ancient spells — "SELECT * FROM users WHERE excitement_level = high" sounds like a delightful incantation, right? In the realm of data, SQL is not just a language; it's a way of life, a badge of honor worn proudly by those who dare venture into the dark corners of their databases. SQL lets you communicate your wishes to the database gods, whether it's retrieving thrilling insights or sacrificing a few rows of data for the greater good.

As you sip your coffee and don your metaphorical wizard's hat, you'll find that mastering querying techniques with SQL is akin to learning a series of magical potions that transform your data from mundane to magnificent. Picture yourself waving your wand — well, cursor — as you conjure up JOINs that unite tables like long-lost friends at a high school reunion. Want to filter out the noise? WHERE clauses are your trusty broomsticks, helping you hover gracefully over unnecessary data and landing softly on just what you need. Grouping data? GROUP BY is like a spell that organizes your chaotic parchment into neat categories that would make any librarian drool with envy. But don't stop there; use aggregate functions like COUNT, SUM, and AVG to become the grand alchemist of your dataset, concocting golden statistics that just might impress Aunt Gertrude at your next family gathering. With SQL by your side, you'll wield data manipulation techniques that make you feel less like a mere analyst and more like an all-knowing sorcerer casting spells in the great hall of insights!

4.2 Promql And Logql: The Secret Spells For Perfect Graphs

PromQL and LogQL are the magical incantations that transform your data into dazzling graphs, akin to how a sorcerer conjures an impressive firework display. These query languages allow you to dive deep into your time-series data and logs with the expertise of a seasoned wizard. PromQL, designed primarily for querying Prometheus data, enables you to pull metrics, aggregate them, and even perform arithmetic operations, turning numbers into visual feasts. As for LogQL, it works its charms on your logs, retrieving essential data and filtering down to the nuggets of wisdom hidden in the chaos, almost like a librarian identifying the exact tome you need in a labyrinthine library. Together, these spells enable you to manipulate data like a puppet master, controlling every aspect of your visualization and making it as stunning as a peacock in full display. Understanding these languages is akin to wielding Excalibur; they grant you the ability to create dashboards adorned with charts that practically leap off the screen.

Now that you've dipped your toes in the enchanting waters of PromQL and LogQL, it's time to practice these incantations like you're prepping for the annual Data Wizards Championship! Picture this: You summon a line chart that elegantly showcases your CPU usage over time, but wait! You find yourself conjuring a graph that looks more like a cat's whiskers than a useful visualization. Fear not! With a pinch of arithmetic in the query and a dash of strategic labeling, that chaotic squiggle transforms into a majestic display of clarity. On the LogQL side, you might discover yourself sifting through logs to find that one error message hidden in the thicket. Using filters and proper selectors, you can pinpoint your way to illuminating insights, like unearthing a buried treasure in a pirate's cove. The more you practice these magical spells, the better you'll become at manifesting visualizations that dazzle, inform, and lead your audience to applaud your wizardry.

As you embark on this journey of querying mastery, remember that the secret lies not only in getting it right but also in the art of experimenting. Each query you try is a step closer to crafting the perfect graph, so keep tweaking, testing, and tailoring your incantations until they shimmer with brilliance. Use Grafana's visual editor as your cauldron, allowing you to mix the ingredients of PromQL and LogQL to bubble up the perfect brew of information that captivates and enlightens your viewers.

4.3 Error 500: When Queries Go South

Error 500—it's like the label on a mystery box that hints at chaos inside but never explains what the ruckus is. When you see this message, it's a sign that your server has unleashed its full potential for melodrama. Perhaps it's sulking in the corner because a query made it sad, or it could be that there's a syntax error lurking in the shadows, just waiting to spoil the party. Whatever the reason, the 500 error indicates that the server hit a snag so deep, even Sherlock Holmes would throw up his hands in frustration. Your queries went south, and now you're left feeling like a parent whose child has just rediscovered how to paint—unfortunately, the medium is your server logs. Dive into those logs like you're on a treasure hunt, because that's where the breadcrumbs of information live, leading you toward the horrid truth about what went wrong. Is it an overflow? A timeout? A drama-filled function that decided to throw an exception without an RSVP? It's your job to play detective and find the root cause, while dodging the occasional existential crisis about your own coding prowess.

Once you've gotten over the mental hurdle caused by that pesky Error 500, it's time to flip the script on querying disasters. Every time a server hiccups and sends you a heart-stopping message, there's an opportunity to learn and grow. Start by adopting a mindset of curiosity rather than panic. Break down each query like a mad scientist examines their experiment. What variables are you introducing? Are they misbehaving like rebellious kittens? Consider using a staging environment for trial runs, giving you the chance to catch issues before they make a grand debut in production. Tighten up those queries, introduce indexing like a wise librarian, and watch performance improve. Keep a tidy workflow, and document your queries with the same zeal that an artist uses to sign their masterpiece. Over time, those query frights will turn into gratifying insights, and you'll be the data wizard pulling insights out of a hat while others are still fumbling with their hats, looking for the rabbit. Always remember, a little humor goes a long way; a chuckle at your missteps can lighten the mood as you conquer those pesky 500 errors one query at a time.

CHAPTER 5 – ALERT! ALERT! PANIC NOT REQUIRED

5.1 Setting Up Alerts: The Art Of Avoiding False Alarms

Strategically setting up alerts is akin to placing a well-timed whoopee cushion on the chair of an unsuspecting friend—one must aim for the perfect moment, ideally when laughter ensues rather than confusion or panic. The trick lies in making your alerts smart enough to know when to sound the alarm bell sensibly, rather than at the mere flicker of a light. This is achieved by targeting specific thresholds that genuinely signify a problem rather than just mild annoyance, such as Bob unplugging a switch because he thought it looked better off. It's all about identifying those pesky incidents that require immediate attention while ignoring the harmless hiccups that can be resolved with a casual shrug and a 'let's not bother anyone with this' attitude. By doing so, you ensure that your alert system doesn't turn into the digital version of a fire-breathing dragon, scaring away the villagers at the slightest rustle of the leaves.

Avoiding the 'boy who cried wolf' scenario is crucial for maintaining sanity on your team and ensuring your alerts are respected rather than dismissed as an overzealous alarmist. There's nothing quite like the sound of a Slack message at 3 AM, causing hearts to race only to realize it's just a low disk space issue from last week's pizza party. The solution? Consistently refine your alerting strategy by tuning the parameters, so they appropriately reflect the criticality of the situation. It may require a bit of trial and error, experimenting with different thresholds, and listening to the whispers in the server logs like a wise oracle, but it's worth it. Designing alerts that only trigger for real emergencies is the key to preserving the peace and keeping your sanity intact. Remember, a good alert is like a trusted friend—always dependable but not unnecessarily alarmist!

Smart alerting isn't just a safety net; it's a way to foster a calm and productive work environment. Avoid a world where alerts act as the digital equivalent of a Melissa McCarthy comedy—funny the first time but downright exhausting if it happens too often. By creating alerts that are both sensible and reassuring, you pave the way for a more efficient workflow. Plus, your colleagues will appreciate the absence of needless panic, letting the team focus on genuine issues that actually require immediate action. The next time you're setting those all-important alerts, think of them not as alarms waiting to scream but as gentle nudges reminding everyone to stay on track without the alarmist theatrics.

5.2 Escalation Policies: Who To Call When The Sky Is Falling

Crafting an effective escalation policy is like writing a sitcom—it involves a good understanding of your cast, the plot, and the big moments when everything could go hilariously wrong. The first step is to clearly define who's on call and ensure they know what they're signing up for. Imagine in the throes of a server meltdown, you mistakenly wake up Uncle Bob instead of Karen from DevOps, who actually knows what to do. Bob, bless him, is there clutching his ice cream, fully prepared to dive into troubleshooting mode but confused about why his phone is ringing—gotta love his dedication. It's important to develop a robust list of roles and their associated responsibilities, providing crystal clear guidelines, so everyone knows precisely what to do when chaos descends. This list should not only include primary contacts but also secondary ones—who doesn't love an understudy ready to swoop in and save the day like a caffeinated superhero?

The art of proper escalation hinges on communication and context. Nobody wants to spring from their slumber, bleary-eyed and disoriented, only to find their phone blasting alerts about something that could have been handled with a quick restart—ideally during daylight hours when their brain has had the chance to warm up. Consider implementing a tiered escalation system where alerts gradually increase in urgency. For instance, if a server is simply grumpy, a gentle nudge via a polite system notification should suffice. If Armageddon is at hand, however, the alert must transform into the digital equivalent of a fire alarm—a loud, blaring "Get your coffee and get up NOW!" alert that could awaken even the most devoted dreamer. The goal here is to eliminate unnecessary nighttime panic. No one, after all, survives a 3 a.m. wakeup call from a chatbot telling them that their SQL query has gone rogue. That's just *not* good for anyone's sanity.

Establishing these guidelines not only protects the night owls from unneeded distress but also curates a sense of teamwork and shared responsibility during crucial moments when everything hits the fan. By fostering an environment of informed communication and clarity during crises, team members can be more equipped to solve issues rather than play the blame game. Remember, when the sky is falling, and Uncle Bob is on speed dial, who you call can make all the difference. So, take some time to craft your escalation policy—it may just keep the panic at bay and your systems humming along quite nicely.

5.3 Keeping Bob Away From The Switch

Bob's curiosity knows no bounds, and when it comes to switches, it's as if he's an ancient explorer seeking hidden treasures. To protect your monitors from Bob's eager fingers, consider implementing a series of clever barriers that would successfully deter even the most relentless sprinter. First, distraction is your best friend. Place a giant rubber ducky or some weirdly amusing desk toy near the workstation. Bob's fascination with the absurd will create a temporary mental detour. Alternatively, you could create an elaborate sign that reads, "DO NOT TOUCH! Powered by unicorn magic" — the very thought of magical consequences may just keep his hands at bay. Use this psychological warfare alongside physical barriers, like a cleverly placed yet impenetrable acrylic box that showcases the switches while still protecting them. This fortress of curiosity will keep Bob's fingers busy in their own flurry of confusion.

Once you've safeguarded the monitors, it's time to establish a 'Bob-proof' zone. This should be a space entirely devoid of anything that might set off his agitated curiosity. Think of it as a highly sophisticated, controlled environment where ordinary monitor activity does not occur. Soft, muted colors are key. Bright colors might trigger that cartoon-like personality of his. Nestle those monitors in a cozy corner filled with plants and beautiful, zen-like décor that creates a serene vibe, making the dashboard seem a tad less enticing. Employ cozy seating nearby and encourage leisurely conversations to redirect discussions away from the workstation. Always remember, the best way to enjoy effective monitoring is to create a space where Bob feels relaxed but entirely disinterested in what's happening with the switches. Like trying to convince a cat to take a bath, it's all about making the alternative seem far more appealing.

Ultimately, controlling Bob is less about barricading the switches and more about outsmarting him with humorous distractions and carefully curated environments. Set the stage for his disinterest with whimsical touches that make the workspace feel more like a coffee shop and less like a command center. Next time he wanders close to the switches, watch as he stops in his tracks, perplexed by the rubber duck's loud quack, while you keep a watchful eye on the monitors to ensure steady operations. A little creativity can turn the chaos of Bob into a delightful spectacle, allowing you to enjoy monitoring without fear of his curious hands flipping critical switches.

CHAPTER 6 – USERS, ROLES, AND THE ART OF CONTROLLED CHAOS

6.1 The Importance Of User Permissions: Who Gets What

User permissions often feel like a riddle wrapped in a mystery inside an enigma, but with a lot more paperwork and headaches. The reality is, everyone loves a good access control drama. Picture it: you're a project manager, innocently trying to assign roles, and suddenly, you find yourself in deep waters. Who gets admin access? Who's allowed to view sensitive data? And why, oh why, does Karen from DevOps insist she needs it all? It's like handing your cat the keys to your car. Sure, they look cute, but you know you'll end up with a shredded steering wheel and fur in places you didn't know existed.

If your user permissions system is more tangled than a ball of yarn in a room full of excited kittens, then it's time to simplify the chaos. Start by defining a clear hierarchy of roles, ensuring everyone knows who can do what. Think of it as a game of Monopoly—only let the players who can handle the chance cards truly participate. By creating distinct roles, like Viewer, Editor, and Admin, you not only avoid confusion but also minimize the risk of catastrophic user-induced disasters. The goal is to maintain order in a place where pandemonium could reign supreme. Remember, controlling user permissions doesn't just help keep the system efficient; it's about saving your sanity too.

6.2 The 'Karen' Exception: When Admin Access Goes Awry

Admin access is like handing a 12-gauge shotgun to a toddler — amusing in theory but terrifying in practice. When teams grant administrative rights without the necessary precautions, chaos can ensue faster than you can say "who broke the server?" Picture Karen from DevOps, armed with her newfound admin powers, unleashed onto the infrastructure like a tornado in a trailer park. Suddenly, her penchant for mischief becomes a grave security concern. She starts adding plugins in a frenzy, convinced she can achieve data visualization nirvana, only to discover that the plugin she installed has turned the server into a digital version of a dumpster fire. Administrators often find themselves recounting stories of users whose exploits transformed ordinary tasks into horror stories that haunt the halls of Slack channels long after the incident. From accidental data deletions to disastrous changes in configuration that leave everyone scratching their heads, the misadventures of those with admin access are legendary. It's a wild world out there, filled with hair-raising tales that could fill a horror anthology, but instead become morning meeting lore.

The rationale for cutting back on who gets admin access is as clear as the murky waters of a neglected fish tank. Limiting privileges isn't about suppressing creativity; it's about controlling the chaos. Just as we wouldn't let a child play with fireworks on a whim, we shouldn't allow everyone in the IT team to wield the all-powerful admin key. Each time a user gains admin rights, it's like inviting an unwieldy elephant into a crowded room — you really don't know if it's going to stomp around or just sit quietly until the end of the meeting. By restricting admin privileges, teams can reduce the risk of unauthorized changes, minimize the impact of mistakes, and prevent rogue plugins from crashing the digital party. It's not that we don't trust our teammates; it's that we're all just one stray click away from a minor apocalypse. Clear roles and defined boundaries create a structured environment where creativity can flourish without setting fire to the entire network. Keep that admin access restricted, and watch how beautifully the chaos transforms into productive teamwork.

6.3 Managing Chaos: Best Practices For User Roles

Managing user roles in your data kingdom is a bit like herding cats — if those cats were also passionate about dashboards and had a propensity to mess with each other's queries. Best practices in this quirky realm of user management can help maintain order amidst the glorious chaos. Start by clearly defining the roles within your team. Not everyone needs admin access, and if you think they do, you probably haven't seen what happens when Dave from Marketing gets his hands on the delete button. You want to assign roles based on necessity, not convenience. For instance, Developers can tinker with the settings and dashboards, but only give the Magic Admin powers to someone who'll use that power wisely — you know, like Karen from DevOps. She gets things done, and she's less likely to accidentally delete the production server. Establishing these hierarchies helps to keep your data kingdom from devolving into a free-for-all where even the janitor could change the database schema.

If chaos theory has taught us anything, it's that misunderstandings are just waiting to happen, much like the flap of a Canadian goose's wings causing a tornado in Kansas. By keeping your team's roles clearer than a perfectly rendered Grafana chart, you not only reduce confusion but also make it easy to point fingers when something breaks — I mean, hold people accountable in a constructive way. When everyone knows who is responsible for what, it saves you from endless "But I thought you were in charge of that!" conversations that usually echo into the void of the never-ending Slack channel debates. Think of it like organizing a rock band where the guitarist knows his solo, the drummer is on beat, and no one is trying to play the tambourine when it's not their turn. Content users with defined responsibilities will lead to a more harmonious data exploration experience, so keep those roles as clear as an alpine lake on a still day — or at least, as clear as the intentions behind Karen's cryptic Slack messages.

For best results, implement a documentation process that outlines specific role definitions and access levels. This newspaper of responsibilities will serve as both a guide and a warning. You can turn it into a buddy-buddy reference for your team or a dramatic play starring the drama of 'Your Access Is Not What You Think' — only without the popcorn. Remember, user roles should be revisited periodically to accommodate shifts in company structure or to introduce shiny new team members who may be chomping at the bit to break things. By maintaining an updated record of who gets to do what, you'll be pretty amazed at how much calmer your data kingdom becomes cutting through the chaos like a hot knife through butter. Effective user role management can turn potential anarchy into a well-oiled machine. Now, if only we could get Canadian geese to follow suit.

CHAPTER 7 – PLUGIN ROULETTE AND OTHER DANGEROUS GAMES

7.1 Responsible Plugin Installation: A Step-By-Step Guide

Plugin installation is like baking a fancy cake; it requires the right ingredients, a sturdy pan, and, above all, a good recipe. Start by checking if your plugin comes from a reputable source. Think of it as ensuring your flour hasn't been used for sock puppetry—quality matters! Get into the habit of reading reviews, checking ratings, and maybe even performing a little spell to ward off potential demons lurking in the code. Once you've found a plugin that seems as trustworthy as a golden retriever at the park, back up your dashboard like you'd back up your most cherished cat photos—because, let's face it, disasters happen faster than you can say 'plugin update.' After backing up your data, prepare your environment. For every plugin, there's a hidden checklist. Make sure your server can handle it, that you're running compatible versions, and that you're equipped with any dependencies. Installing a plugin meant for a 1999 operating system on a new server is like trying to fit a VHS tape into a streaming service—futile and potentially tragic.

When venturing into plugin territory, think before you leap. Overloading your darling dashboard with plugins is like inviting every acquaintance from high school to your birthday party; it might feel fun at first, but it quickly turns into chaos. Each plugin added is like another friend requesting to borrow your favorite hoodie. Some are perfectly respectful; others will return it covered in nacho cheese. Quiz each plugin with some basic questions: What features does it offer? How frequently is it updated? Does the developer provide decent support or just a newsletter filled with dad jokes? In the end, select plugins that not only dazzle you but bring real value and won't turn your server into a cold-pizza dumpster from which there is no recovery. Keeping your setup lean means quicker loading times and fewer chances of getting tangled in error logs that resemble a modern art piece gone wrong. If you find yourself in trouble, look up the documentation —just think of it as consulting the wise old sage of plugin installation, dishing out wisdom like it's hot cocoa on a winter's day.

7.2 Irresponsible Plugin Choices: Tales From The Error Log

Imagine this: It's a bright sunny afternoon in the world of database administration, and you've just decided to give your Grafana dashboard a facelift. You're scrolling through the plethora of plugins, eyes glinting with excitement like a kid in a candy store. But beware, for choice can be a double-edged sword! One poor soul—let's call him Dave from IT—once decided it was a brilliant idea to install a plugin that promised to "supercharge" his visualizations overnight. But instead of picturesque panels, he ended up with a chaotic mess that looked more like a toddler's finger-painting gone awry. The error logs were screaming, his Slack notifications resembled a frantic choir, and suddenly, Dave found himself lost in a sea of broken graphs and spinning loading icons. As he sat in front of his screen, the horror of the situation dawned on him: the "supercharged" plugin had supercharged his frustration levels instead. Tales like Dave's are sprinkled across the internet like breadcrumbs leading to a dark howling void known as the error log.

So, what can we glean from these cautionary tales? First and foremost, tread carefully when selecting plugins. Ensure they are well-documented, regularly updated, and have a reputation for being reliable. Understand that just because a plugin has a shiny icon and enticing promises doesn't mean it won't bite you like a puppy with a shoe obsession. The right plugin should enhance your experience, not turn your dashboard into a digital horror show. Picture this: a wise mentor once quipped, "Be wary of the plugin that arrives with lightning bolts and fire-breathing dragons." This sage advice rings true, especially when your emergency alert at 3 AM points to that flashy, untested, brand-new plugin you installed after three cups of coffee and too many optimistic messages. Always remember: it's not just about adding flashy features; it's about maintaining harmony. When in doubt, consult the error log before it becomes a verbose dictionary of your mistakes, and keep those plugins in line like well-behaved pets at the dog park. In the end, choosing wisely could save your sanity—along with a couple of MacBooks—down the road.

7.3 Finding The Perfect Balance: Plugin Management Strategies

Striking a balance with plugins is like trying to juggle flaming swords while riding a unicycle—easy to mess up, but oh-so-rewarding when you nail it. Imagine your dashboard is a symphony orchestra and each plugin is an instrument; too many violins can make for a cacophony, while too few can leave your audience yawning. The key is to enhance productivity without drowning in a sea of notifications or alarms. By carefully selecting plugins that serve specific purposes—like a tireless sous-chef handling only the most essential tasks—you can transform your dashboard from a crowded space into a streamlined powerhouse. Instead of flailing wildly at every new shiny plugin, take your time to evaluate each one. If it doesn't add significant value to your workflow or isn't absolutely essential, give it a merry wave goodbye and let it exit stage left, ideally without crashing your system in the process!

Now that you've decided which plugins to keep, let's talk strategies for managing them with the elegance of a well-practiced magician. One effective approach is treating your plugins like house guests: each needs to be invited in, given a specific purpose, and monitored closely to ensure they don't take too long in the bathroom or command too much of your attention. This means regularly reviewing what's installed, assessing their impact, and getting rid of those pesky plugins that have overstayed their welcome. Another tactic involves organizing your plugins into categories that make sense to your workflow—grouping those that enhance performance, usability, and visual appeal. Having a neat little system in place to document their purpose and settings can save you time and headaches down the line, especially when they start fighting for screen space like rival rock bands at a music festival. When the chaos of plugin overload threatens to disrupt your serene coding Zen, you'll be a lot better off with your carefully curated selections and proper management. Consider creating a simple chart or note to track any inter-plugin quirks and conflicts, making future troubleshooting as smooth as that first sip of coffee.

In the wild world of plugin managment, keep your workflow tidy and intentional. Consider a method similar to "spring cleaning." That's right—don't just install plugins like they're going out of style; approach your dashboard like a curator in a museum, showcasing only the finest pieces. By establishing a regular check-up routine for your plugins, removing the outdated ones, and keeping a finely-tuned balance, you turn your dashboard into an efficient workhorse rather than a cluttered garage. This could involve setting aside about 30 minutes each month to review, uninstall, or update plugins, making it easier to enjoy the ride instead of wrestling with the chaos. With your plugins in perfect harmony, you'll find you can accomplish tasks like a caffeinated cheetah, avoiding distractions and keeping productivity levels soaring!

CHAPTER 8 – A BACKUP WALKS INTO A BAR...

8.1 Disaster Recovery Planning: Don't Be Caught Unprepared

A disaster recovery plan is like an Escape Room for IT incidents. Imagine being in a room full of servers, data, and the inexplicable dread of potential doom. You've got to plan your way out before the masked figure of disaster shows up, and trust me, it shows up without an invitation. The goal is to have a fancy cheat sheet that can guide you through the chaos. Start by clearly outlining the possible disasters you could encounter. Is it an epic power failure, data corruption, or perhaps a zombie apocalypse led by the dev team? You need to identify and categorize these potential disasters like you're assembling a superhero team, each with their unique powers and weaknesses. Then, detail the steps on how to combat each calamity. Document every procedure like you're writing a manual for a time machine! Specify who handles what; assign roles like you're casting for a sitcom. Remember, it's not just about saving the day—it's about making it look good while you're at it. Finally, test this plan repeatedly until the only tears shed are from laughter, not panic. This ensures that you're perpetually one step ahead, in the disaster planning game.

Knowledge is your trusty sidekick in the battle against disasters.

Equip yourself like a wizard preparing for a duel—except instead of wands and spells, you have knowledge bases, training sessions, and maybe a couple of tech blogs as your charms. Start with gaining insight into your systems. Know which data sits where, and how it interacts like a tangled sitcom family. Familiarize yourself with the various recovery tools available because there's a difference between an IT guru and a person who is frantically looking for the "undo" button. Join forums, attend seminars, and keep your ear to the ground for the latest in tech trends. This way, you'll be ready to face any digital calamity that dares cross your path—whether it's a rogue query that thinks it's fun to eat all the memory or an unexpected storage collapse. Remember, in the turmoil of disaster recovery, the calm, collected individual with the most knowledge will emerge not only victorious but also quite possibly hilariously self-satisfied after keeping their cool. Consider adopting a motto, like: "Backup today, or face a Sherwood Forest of lost data tomorrow!"

8.2 The Farce Of Sqlite In Production: A Cautionary Tale

Using SQLite in production is often compared to a firework show that goes hilariously awry. Picture it: the vibrant explosions lighting up the sky, everyone oohing and aahing, until bam! A rogue firework veers off course, igniting a nearby tree and sending spectators running in every direction. SQLite is like that enthusiastic firework; it's charming and easy to set up, but when the real pressure hits, it can transform from a fan favorite into a chaotic scene. The simplicity that makes SQLite appealing in development can lead to catastrophic failures in a production environment. It is designed for lightweight, local scenarios and when it gets thrust into the high-stakes arena of production, it quickly starts to show its limitations like a clown car in a race. Just because it works on your laptop doesn't mean it has the chops for managing hefty transaction loads, concurrent writes, or the demands of a bustling web application.

Understanding the limitations of databases is crucial in the tech world. While SQLite is fantastic for prototyping and small-scale applications, it lacks the robust features of more powerful databases like PostgreSQL or MySQL. For instance, SQLite has a locking mechanism that can lead to bottlenecks during high concurrency, so if you thought your app could handle a surge of users querying at the same time, think again! Each write operation can lock the whole database, making you feel like you're in a waiting room for an important appointment—except the doctor forgot you're there. Best practices dictate a thorough evaluation of your database needs before deployment. This means exploring options that provide better scalability, reliability, and concurrent user handling. Save SQLite for development, small applications, or where a single user is involved, and let the other heavyweights take the main stage in production. Your future self will thank you when the users are happily clicking away and not screaming at you to fix the dumpster fire that was once your SQLite database.

Remember, the key to a successful production environment isn't just choosing the right database, but also being aware of best practices. This includes proper backups, monitoring, and opting for solutions that allow for recovery plans when things go awry. Never let the cute, friendly appeal of a simple SQLite setup convince you to take a dangerously optimistic leap into production. Approach database choices with the caution of a cat surveying a puddle—observant, skeptical, and calculating your next move to avoid an unexpected drenching.

8.3 Restoring Data: Tips For A Smooth Process

The world of data restoration can often feel like assembling IKEA furniture with missing parts and vague instructions. However, armed with the right tips, you can transform what seems to be an apocalyptic disaster into a graceful ballet of bits and bytes. First and foremost, clarity is your best friend. Ensure you have a clear plan that outlines every step of the restoration process, because without a map, you might accidentally restore a backup from 2012 that contains more cat memes than actual data.

One of the golden rules of restoration is to test your backups regularly. Think of it as checking the expiration date on your yogurt; just because it's been sitting in the fridge doesn't mean it's still good. If your backups don't restore properly, it's time to head back to the drawing board with your backup strategy. Furthermore, when the moment of truth arrives and you're finally ready to perform the restoration, don't forget the power of incremental backups. These small saviors can save you mega time, ensuring that you're not reinstalling an entire database filled with data from last Tuesday when you just needed to grab that one report from yesterday. Plus, they throw in all the benefits of fewer headaches.

The dreaded restore process is where nerves run high, but it doesn't have to be a horror movie. Channel your inner pro, and approach this like a well-rehearsed musical number rather than an unscripted improv night. Before hitting the 'restore' button, make sure you've got your tools in hand—documentation, checklists, and maybe a fresh cup of coffee for the nerves. More importantly, ensure you're in a quiet, distraction-free zone; nothing derails a restore quite like Greg in Marketing blaring his playlist at full volume.

If you're feeling fancy, consider using scripts to automate parts of your restoration process. Scripts are like trade secrets that only the cool kids in the tech playground know; they can help accelerate the restore process faster than you can say "SQL injection." Automation also prevents human-induced typos, proving that while humans may err, scripts are relentless perfectionists. And if it all goes sideways, remember: staying cool under pressure is key. Breathe, laugh a little, and remind yourself that you're navigating the wild world of data like the expert you are, even if you're secretly sweating bullets. And here's a nugget of wisdom: always have a contingency plan. Just in case the restoration process turns into a journey of epic proportions, an emergency backup strategy prepared in advance can save the day and spare you from future meltdowns.

CHAPTER 9 – HIGH AVAILABILITY OR HIGH ANXIETY?

9.1 Understanding High Availability (Ha) Setups

High Availability (HA) setups sound like something out of a sci-fi movie, perhaps featuring robots that serve your coffee while ensuring that your website never goes down. But let's demystify this all-important concept. HA setups typically consist of multiple systems working together seamlessly, like a well-rehearsed dance troupe. Imagine a stage where if one dancer trips over their shoelace, another one tiptoes in to help without missing a beat. This redundancy is crucial; it allows services to keep running smoothly even when a component decides it's had enough and checks out for an extended vacation. Making sure your application can withstand individual failures is like having a bouncer at a club to ensure that only the best dancers hit the stage, and everyone else just has to sit out for a while until they're ready to perform again. Ultimately, HA setups are a blend of clever design and skilled engineering.

Now, while the idea of having a service that's always available sounds fantastic—like a pizza delivery that always arrives in under 10 minutes—it does come with its own quirky complications. The balance between uptime and complexity can often feel like trying to juggle flaming torches while riding a unicycle. For every redundant server you add, you introduce potential points of failure, configurations that need babysitting, and perhaps the odd network latency that feels like it's directly poking you in the eye. While striving for 99.9999% uptime (which you'll hear referred to as five nines, though I wouldn't recommend counting to that with your fingers), remember that sometimes, less really is more. Implementing a simpler strategy might mean sacrificing a few precious nines but can give you a much more manageable setup. So think carefully about what you actually need to ensure that your services are available, without getting lost in a messy web of complexity that resembles a kindergarten art project gone awry. A good rule of thumb? Simplify your infrastructure unless you have a serious craving for chaos.

9.2 Sharing Databases Without Losing Your Mind

Sharing databases is a delicate dance, sort of like twirling a flaming baton while balancing on a unicycle. The moment you throw in someone else's opinions, expectations, and bizarre SQL queries, the whole performance could turn into a circus act. To prevent your database from becoming a nightmarish monster, consider using clear access levels. Designate who can view, edit, and share data. Think of this as creating a club where only the cool kids with the right credentials can enter, leaving the chaos outside. Set up a policy about how data should be shared; for example, establish a "Read-Only Friday" or perhaps "No Querying at Midnight," which might save a few employees from accidentally unleashing SQL Kraken while feeling inspired by an extra cup of coffee.

Remember, etiquette matters more than you think. Establishing norms, like using comment sections for queries or providing a quick overview of recent changes in a shared document, can save everyone a lot of time and discomfort. A communal calendar or a shared Slack channel where good news and tips flow just like caffeine at a Monday morning meeting can make sharing seamless and spark joy—kind of like a buddy cop duo, just without the high-speed chases. Frequent check-ins for feedback could help you gauge if you're still on the same page, preventing the great "Who Moved My Cheese?" crisis that happens when standards drift apart.

Database sharing etiquette is like the unwritten rules of the office fridge: don't take someone else's food, label your leftovers, and for heaven's sake, clean up any mess you make. Adopt a similar mindset when handling databases. Proper naming conventions are your best friend—avoid cryptic titles like "Final_Version_2_NoReallyThisIsTheFinal.docx." Instead, use descriptive, organized names that could help anyone find what they're after faster than a cat chasing a laser pointer. This simple tweak not only saves precious moments but could also prevent emotional outbursts fueled by confusion.

And let's talk about documentation, because a well-written guide can feel like a comforting hug after a long day. Include key data sharing procedures, explanations of complex queries, or even just what the heck that one random column represents. Good documentation is like a life preserver thrown into the stormy sea of queries—embrace it! Finally, encourage a collaborative spirit by exchanging tips on querying efficiently. This creates an enjoyable environment where knowledge flows like free snacks at a tech meetup, fostering camaraderie instead of competition. So go on, share that database, but remember the golden rule: keep it as drama-free as possible.

9.3 The Choral Symphonies Of Grafana-Server Processes

Reveling in the ambiance created by multiple grafana-server processes can feel like you're at a concert of harmony, with each process playing its own unique part yet contributing to the symphony of data visualization. Imagine each grafana-server as a talented musician, finely tuned and ready to deliver an exhilarating performance. When they work together seamlessly, it's as if they're singing a melodic tune that presents your data in a way that dancers (or in this case, users) can enjoy. The rhythm of successful queries and the crescendo of well-timed alerts create a digital masterpiece that keeps chaos at bay. But watch closely! Just like any band, if one grafana-server is out of tune—say, if it forgets to share a critical piece of information—the harmony can quickly turn into cacophony, swinging through frenetic highs and desperate lows. The art lies in orchestration, ensuring each process plays its designated role while harmonizing with the others to keep the visualization concert a delightful experience.

To ensure your HA setup sings beautifully, rather than producing discordant chaos, it is crucial to master the art of configuration. Picture this: a server setup that resembles a well-rehearsed choir, where every process knows when to jump in and when to hang back. A high-availability setup should have redundancy baked right in, giving you a comforting layer of backup and support. It's all about balance and ensuring that your primary and standby processes can perform their tasks without stepping on each other's toes. This way, if one server process decides to take a little unscheduled nap, the others won't miss a beat. Keep an eye on those logs, conduct regular tune-ups, and watch closely for any signs of disharmony. By treating each grafana-server like a vital member of your ensemble, you turn your entire monitoring system into a melodious experience that everyone will want to hear—and best of all, it keeps your end users from discovering the joys of chaos.

CHAPTER 10 – THE DASHBOARD GRAVEYARD

10.1 Organizing Dashboards: Folders And Tags For Sanity

Organizing dashboards is a secret art form that many have tried and few have mastered. The first step to achieving this zen state involves recognizing the so-called "graveyard effect." Picture a dark, cavernous space filled with creepy, half-forgotten dashboards gathering digital dust like ancient relics. Every once in a while, you might stumble upon one, but trying to remember who made it or why is akin to deciphering hieroglyphs in a computer science museum. To combat this, create a structured hierarchy of folders where every dashboard gets a proper home. Group similar dashboards together, perhaps even naming folders with humorous titles that resonate with your team. Use names like Metrics Madness or Graphs Gone Wild to keep the mood light while ensuring nobody accidentally ends up wandering into the dashboard graveyard. Your dashboards deserve better than a fate where they languish in obscurity!

Now, let's talk about tagging. Tagging like a pro can save your dashboards from becoming lost in the abyss of your folder structure. Imagine both your dashboard and your sanity rely on a robust tagging system. Think of tags as the bright neon signs in a murky forest—they guide the way! Create tags that reflect the contents, functionality, and purpose of each dashboard. Be specific and creative! Instead of just "Sales" or "Finance," go wild with something like "CashFlow Carnival" or "Penny Pinchers Paradise." If you find yourself dealing with dashboards that serve multiple purposes, don't hesitate to layer on the tags. Just like a good nacho plate, the more toppings, the better! This way, even if a dashboard drifts off to an unknown folder, a quick search for its tags will bring it back to you faster than a cat to a sunny spot. Proper organization and tagging are the twin pillars that will keep you from being buried alive in a sea of dashboards.

10.2 Version Control: Keeping Track Of Changes

Version control is like the magic wand of dashboard management. Picture this: You stumble upon a pie chart that you absolutely adore, only to find out later that it's based on data from 2019, when everyone thought low-fat yogurt was a food group. With version control, you can keep your historical data intact while ensuring that the current version of your dashboard sings the freshest tunes. It tracks every little change, every tweak, and every 'oops that wasn't supposed to go live,' allowing you to revert back to an earlier version faster than you can say "data integrity." When you accidentally delete those glowing metrics for last quarter, a quick rollback keeps the party going without sending your team into panic mode. Consider version control your dashboard's trusty sidekick, always there to save the day from catastrophic disasters, like a cat jumping on your keyboard right as you're about to hit 'Save.'

Who doesn't love a little friendly collaboration? The problem arises when your team members are playing a game of "who can mess up the dashboard the fastest" without even knowing it. Imagine the horror of presenting the latest metrics and finding a series of graphs that look more like abstract art than actual data! Versioning comes to the rescue like a superhero in spandex, allowing everyone to contribute while keeping track of individual changes. Think of it as a big collaborative mural where each stroke is carefully noted, and if someone decides to paint a completely different picture, you can just roll back to the moment before they picked up the brush. This not only fosters teamwork but also prevents you from having to explain why the department is suddenly trending in a completely new direction because of Bob's 'creative' interpretation of sales data. By embracing version control, you create a harmonious environment where mistakes get addressed, innovations happen, and you can avoid the dreaded situation of redraws during crucial meetings. Reporting can go from cringeworthy to confident with just a click.

10.3 Dealing With Legacy Dashboards: The 2019 Anomaly

Legacy dashboards are like that one relative who overstayed their welcome at Thanksgiving dinner, still hanging around your analytics platform long after they've ceased to be useful. You know the ones: they're the dashboards created in 2019 that nobody wants to admit they were responsible for, festooned with outdated metrics and ancient queries that look like they were designed before the invention of the internet. These relics often hold the weight of nostalgia, sitting smugly in folders with names like ASAP Charts or Must-Have Metrics—ironically, they do not qualify as either anymore.

Identifying these dashboard leftovers isn't just about a slow crawl through a digital graveyard; it requires an adventurous spirit like that of a treasure hunter, albeit one armed with sarcasm and a slightly defunct sense of ethics. Find yourself asking probing questions: "When was the last time anyone looked at this?" and "Who thought a donut chart was a relevant visualization for sales projections?" Understanding their existence is crucial, as these dashboards can drain both your server resources and your sanity. They just sit there, looking pretty, while the real-time data whizzes past them, seemingly mocking your inability to let go.

Cleaning house is never easy, especially when it involves tearing down the crumbling legacy of your dashboard empire. Instead of burning it all down like an angry viking, consider a structured approach. Start with a ruthless audit, channeling your inner organizational guru. Rank your dashboards according to usefulness, relevance, and that old-fashioned gut feeling—does this thing still bring joy or has it become an ugly reminder of a forgotten goal? Consider taking each dashboard on a testing journey, perhaps having a meeting where stakeholders weigh in. If nobody wants to defend it like it's their side of a family feud, you know it's time to put that dashboard out to pasture.

When the axe finally falls, don't just delete; make it a memorable farewell! Archive those poor dashboards that actually contributed something at one point, or at least write a mock eulogy, complete with a heartfelt anecdote about the glory days when everyone believed "more data equals better decisions." Embrace the fact that cleaning house is part of evolution, and it paves the way for innovation within your workspace. Transitioning into sleek, modern dashboards doesn't have to feel like a mid-life crisis; with the right humor and strategy, it can be a liberating experience. And remember, there's nothing like a freshly decluttered dashboard folder to make you feel like the digital Marie Kondo of your organization!

CHAPTER 11 – TEMPLATING AND OTHER BLACK MAGIC

11.1 Understanding Variables: The Power Within

When it comes to dashboards, variables are like the magical wands that transform a static view into a dynamic powerhouse. You take a regular dashboard, maybe with its usual metrics like CPU usage or memory consumption, and suddenly—BAM! —you turn it into a living, breathing display of real-time data adaptability. Imagine a scenario where instead of hardcoding the same metrics over and over, you can tweak them with a simple dropdown. Suddenly, your users feel like they're part of the data-nerd elite, with the power to customize their own views. By using variables, you can allow users to choose time frames, filter by specific teams, or even dive deep into the metrics related to that one server that's always up to no good. The adaptability it brings to dashboards is akin to giving your analytics a shot of espresso— just enough to make them jittery with excitement, while keeping things under control.

Imagine unlocking a treasure chest filled with dynamic capabilities, where each variable is like a glittering gem bursting with potential. With the right variables in hand, ordinary dashboards can morph into extraordinary portals of insight. Want to see how your sales numbers stack up by region, or perhaps compare server performance over different time periods? Bam! With a quick click and some variable wizardry, you've catapulted your dashboard from basic to breathtaking. These variables not only give a zest for interactivity but also invite a world of possibilities. It's like transforming a pumpkin into a dazzling carriage; with a little bit of crafting and a few clever variables, you'll have your dashboard galloping through data like a pro. So, put on your data wizard hat, wield those variables with glee, and watch as your once-stuffy dashboards spring to life with the pizzazz of a disco ball at a '70s party. Always remember, the more variables you wield, the further you can stretch the imaginations of your users—and let's be honest, they do love a bit of pizzazz.

To maximize the potential of your dashboards, consider incorporating regex filters and custom queries. They might sound like spells from a magical text, but with some practice, you'll find they greatly enhance your ability to tailor data presentations to users' whims. Every time you tweak variable settings, imagine you're orchestrating a symphony where every note resonates with relevance.

11.2 Regex Filters: The Wizards Of Data Transformation

Regular expressions, or regex for short, are like the magical wands of the coding universe. They possess the ability to perform complex string manipulations, transforming mere text into whatever shape you desire. Imagine this scenario: you've entered a realm where a data sorcerer like yourself can summon specific pieces of information from a seemingly endless sea of characters, just by uttering the right incantation! Regex allows you to match patterns, find mystical string sequences, and even extract the exact spells you need - all while confounding your peers, who still rely on basic string functions like it's 1999. Remember, regex has a learning curve sharper than a dragon's tooth, but once you've grasped its powers, you'll feel like a wizard casting spells with poise and precision.

Now that you've dipped your toes in this enchanting realm, let's get practical. It's time to embrace your inner wizard and start utilizing regex to filter and shape your data with wizard-like precision. Here, you unleash a fusion of symbols and syntax to form patterns like a master chef blends ingredients. Looking to extract all the email addresses from a soggy document cluttered with text? Fear not! A mere string such as /\b[A-Za-z0-9._%+-]+@[A-Za-z0-9.-]+\.[A-Z|a-z]{2,}\b/ will conjure forth these elusive nuggets of information. Just toss that regex potion into your favorite programming language or data manipulation tool, and voilà! The emails will appear quicker than you can say "abracadabra!"

Armed with regex, you can filter data like a seasoned pro, cleaning up messy datasets with a sprinkle of syntax magic. Want to remove all extraneous whitespace from your data? A swift regex escape like /\s+/ will wipe those sneaky spaces away faster than a broomstick in the hands of a skilled witch. When your dashboards look like a rainbow of confusion, regex can transform a tangled mess into organized beauty – just like a makeover montage in a feel-good movie. By incorporating these patterns, you'll navigate the treacherous waters of data transformation with flair and finesse. So go ahead, unleash your regex skills on your data, and watch as it bends to your will like a well-trained llama.

11.3 Crafting Custom Dashboards: The Training Of A Llama

Imagine if your dashboard had the grace and charm of a well-trained llama. It would take your data and prance around with it, showing you exactly what you need without biting your shins or running off into the sunset. This is where custom templates come into play. Think of templates as your trusty llama wrangler, keeping everything in check and ensuring that your visualizations don't turn into an unruly stampede of numbers and graphs. By customizing your dashboard templates, you can create a unique layout that fits your workflow like a glove, or in this case, like a llamaskin mobile carrier. Say goodbye to one-size-fits-all templates that make your data look like mashed potatoes after a food fight. Instead, embrace the beauty of tailored designs that make your critical metrics shine in all their glory.

Getting started with customized templates is easier than training a llama to do a dance number. You'll want to first determine what information is most crucial for you and then design your dashboard around that. Are you tracking performance metrics? Customer feedback? How many times your cat has interrupted your workflow? Identify your key variables and layout preferences to develop a structure that tells a cohesive story. Keep in mind, llamas are sleek - so optimize your dashboard for clarity and efficiency. With a little elbow grease, you'll create a visual experience that doesn't just deliver data but provides insights at a glance, all without needing a sherpa to guide you through the terrain.

The magic of dashboard creation often lies in the details. The artistry is all about ensuring that every panel, every graph, and every catchy llama pun serves a purpose. Consider this: anyone can slap together some random graphs and call it a dashboard, but it takes a true artist to craft a visual masterpiece. Knowing how to choose colors that pop like a pinata at a birthday party or mix panel types that communicate rather than clash is where the zany fun really begins. As tempting as it might be to create an explosion of every conceivable metric, focusing on what truly matters will make your insights resonate loftier than a llama at a petting zoo.

Instead of drowning your viewers in data deluge, curate your dashboard like a fine wine tasting, where each ounce reflects the essence of your goals. This means embracing the advanced features available in Grafana or whichever tool you're wielding like a trusty sidekick. Make use of custom queries, variables, and even regex filters that let your metrics dance and sing, pulling in only the most relevant data that tells your story in vibrant detail. The end result? A dashboard that feels less like a college thesis and more like an interactive exhibit at a top-tier zoo. So go ahead, unleash your creativity, channel your inner dashboard artist, and before you know it, your data will be parading across the screen like an esteemed troupe of llamas in their Sunday best.

Remember, a well-crafted dashboard is not just about displaying data – it's about making it a visual joyride. Keep iterating over your designs, solicit feedback, and don't be afraid to tweak features until your dashboard not only serves your needs but also dazzles the eyes involved in the viewing party.

CHAPTER 12 – MONITORING THE MONITOR

12.1 Why Grafana Needs Its Own Caretaker

Grafana, the ever-optimistic data visualization superstar, likes to think of itself as invincible. After all, it happily aggregates data from an endless parade of sources, displaying vivid charts and eye-popping dashboards like a caffeinated magician. However, just like any overzealous entertainer, Grafana has its limits and sometimes requires a little tender loving care—or as we in the industry like to say, a dose of good ol' TLC. Without proper monitoring and maintenance, your beloved Grafana can become sluggish, confused, and might even start throwing tantrums, yielding error messages that sound suspiciously like moans. If your Grafana was a toddler, it would certainly compete for the Oscar in melodrama.

Understanding that Grafana can't run on caffeine alone is crucial. Despite its ability to handle multiple queries and display real-time data with finesse, if left unattended, it risks encountering performance decay faster than a soda left open overnight. Factors such as cache size, unexpected data loads, and asynchronous requests can all lead Grafana down the dark path of emotional distress—err... I mean, technical failure. Setup a regular schedule for updates, ensure the data sources are performing optimally, and most importantly, give Grafana the attention it craves. Think of it as your high-maintenance pet: feed it, pet it, and it likely won't chew your furniture and run away during a storm.

Setting up a monitoring strategy for Grafana might feel like reinventing the wheel, but it's more like ensuring the wheel doesn't turn into a square after a long drive down a bumpy road. Grafana monitoring means keeping tabs on not just its performance metrics but also user interactions, query execution times, and alerting systems. An effective strategy requires vigilance akin to a hawk stalking its prey—or at least like your grandma keeping one eye on the oven when you bake cookies. Start by leveraging Grafana's built-in alerts that notify you if performance metrics exceed predefined thresholds, but don't be that person who sets the bar so low that even a light sneeze triggers panic.

Additionally, employing another monitoring tool can ensure that Grafana itself isn't spiraling into a chaotic abyss. Consider deploying Prometheus alongside Grafana to collect metrics about Grafana's health. When Grafana feels supported by this complement of tools, it can handle a data surge better than a bouncer at a crowded club. Keep logs of query performance and status codes so that when things go south, you don't end up playing 'Where's Waldo' with errors. By implementing a robust monitoring strategy, you ensure your dashboards remain bright, informative, and—most importantly—calm, allowing your efforts to decorate the plain walls of your data universe like a vibrant mural. Just remember, a happy Grafana means a happy you!

12.2 Setting Up Monitoring For Grafana: A Meta Journey

Monitoring Grafana can be as riveting as watching paint dry, but fear not! This is a thrilling odyssey where you become the knight armed with metrics instead of a sword. Picture yourself riding into the wilds of data visualization; your faithful dashboard, Grafana, awaits you with its bright colors and mystical graphs. However, like any noble steed, Grafana requires a bit of care and attention to keep it galloping along smoothly. Start by plotting a path to your monitoring adventures, ensuring you secure the right tools for your quest. Tools like Prometheus, or even Grafana's very own built-in alerting system, will be your trusted sidekicks. As you embark on this journey, make sure your dashboard gets the undivided affection it deserves lest it grow melancholy and crash to the ground like a rogue piñata. You want Grafana to shimmer and shine, not sulk in the corner like a rejected pie chart.

Grafana isn't just any old graphing tool; it's the prima donna of monitoring dashboards. To help it shine like the diamond it is, you must first understand its unique requirements. Begin with the basics—ensure your data sources are both plentiful and reliable, because Grafana won't render magic if it has nothing to work with. Your queries need to sing harmoniously together, creating the symphony of data delights. Be mindful of the time zones, as they can turn a well-planned presentation into a chaos of data misalignment. Grafana thrives on visualization; it relishes in a rich variety of panels and options, all crafted to turn your data into eye candy. But beware—the interference of poorly written queries could send that eye candy tumbling into the abyss of visual confusion. The trick here is to pamper Grafana with clean, well-structured data, avoiding the nightmares of data latency or corruption. So, arm yourself with knowledge and love for your dashboard, and it will return the favor by delighting you with insights that make your data sing.

12.3 Troubleshooting Grafana Failures: Common Pitfalls

Many hilariously common pitfalls lead to Grafana failures, and trust me, the backstories are as amusing as the errors themselves. Picture the time when Jessica from marketing decided to showcase "real-time" data on her pet rock collection. With all the fervor of a caffeinated squirrel, she enthusiastically refreshed the dashboard every two minutes, not realizing that each refresh meant three more alerts about the apparent spikes in CPU usage. The server, lovingly named Carl, was not prepared for this. Then there's good old Bob, who confidently connected Grafana to the unspecified cosmic data source he lovingly crafted during a coffee-fueled all-nighter. Too bad his "data source" was a long-forgotten SQL database named "FlavorTown" containing nothing but spaghetti recipes—oh, the horror when those charts started looking more like a chef's hat than actionable insights. Everyone learned a valuable lesson: when in doubt, always check your data source...and the snacks in the breakroom.

When troubleshooting Grafana meltdowns, transform that initial panic into a zen-like calm with a few handy hacks. First, breathe deeply as you chant, "It's just a data visualization tool; no one is actually going to die." Next, remember the mystical power of the cache-clearing incantation. If your dashboards aren't fetching the latest data, clear that cache like the tidiest of housekeepers. And let's not forget the magical debugging tools embedded within Grafana—it's like having a wizard's staff to poke and prod your queries to see where they went astray. Ask yourself, "Is my query a Shakespearean tragedy, or a comedy of errors?" and devise a game plan accordingly. Also, enlist your secret weapon: the Grafana community forums! They are a fountain of wisdom and shared misadventures that can make even the darkest Grafana hour feel like an episode of your favorite sitcom. Keeping a sense of humor while looking up those error codes goes a long way, not just for your sanity, but your coworkers' as well.

CHAPTER 13 – GRAFANA VS. THE END USERS

13.1 The User Experience: Understanding Dashboard Interaction

The user experience is like a charming prom date; it can be fabulous when it shines, but if it ends up being awkward, nobody will remember the night for the right reasons. In the world of dashboards, user experience often gets lost in translation, like a bad game of Telephone. You design a sleek, intuitive dashboard, complete with dynamic panels and color-coded metrics, but somehow, users are banging their heads on their desks, lost in a sea of graphs and gauges. Why does this happen? It's simple: somewhere in the design process, someone forgot to ask, What do the users actually want? They end up with a symphony of confusing visuals that resemble a pixelated Rorschach test rather than the actionable insights they were hoping for.

Enhancing dashboards means strapping on our proverbial guessing goggles and trying to anticipate user behaviors like a wizard trying to read the future in a crystal ball. This isn't just about flashy graphs that look great on a Monday morning; it's about functional designs that work for every user type, from the seasoned data-analyst magician to the confused intern scrambling to impress their boss. By empathizing with users, we can create something that feels less like an obstacle course and more like a friendly guide to the data universe. Imagine a dashboard that nudges users toward the insights they need, kind of like a barista calling, "Hey, don't forget your whipped cream!" on a complicated order. Predicting their clicks, their scrolls, and even their puzzled frown lines can make dashboards not just a tool, but a delightful experience that users can't wait to interact with daily.

So, when sketching the next masterpiece on your digital canvas, forget the glitter and the gadgets for a moment; listen to the users' unfiltered feedback. Their brainwaves might hold the key to unlocking that coveted ah-ha! moment of clarity that makes for beautiful dashboard interactivity. If you can anticipate user behavior as well as a magician predicts card tricks, you'll have a dashboard that users truly love. Implementing these insights means adding layers of functionality, refining the design into something both delightful and meaningful—a dashboard that doesn't just present data but becomes a haven for decision-making without the maddening rollercoaster of confusion. Remember, the aim here is to create an experience that transforms data panic into data joy.

13.2 The 'Click Everything' Phenomenon: A Case Study

Welcome to the chaotic world of 'click-happy' users, where every button on your dashboard is merely a suggestion and every panel is an invitation to a wild adventure. These users bear an unparalleled enthusiasm for dashboard interaction. They click on everything, as if the mouse were a magical wand that might reveal hidden treasures within the digital landscape you've crafted. Unfortunately, this cavalier attitude towards clicking often results in a tornado of chaos, leaving your once-beautiful dashboards looking like a haphazard collage of messy configurations and broken queries. It seems that with every enthusiastic click, another layer of confusion is added, leading to alarmingly intricate web pages that would make even an origami master sweat. Your Slack channels become inundated with questions such as, Why did my pie chart turn into a bar chart? or Who unleashed the Kraken on my metrics? As if transforming data visualization wasn't enough, these click-happy adventurers embark on a quest to use every filter, drill-down, and refresh button without understanding the consequences. The result is a mix of childish delight and mild panic for the dashboard administrator.

Coping with the whims of click-happy users requires a masterclass in the art of intuitive design. First and foremost, consider constructing your dashboards with user flows that gently guide users toward important actions while subtly discouraging reckless clicking. This could be as simple as a clear hierarchy of data where the most critical metrics shine like the sun, while less important features blend into the shadows—think of it as the "light it up, tone it down" effect. Adding tooltips can provide guidance without overwhelming users or leading them down a rabbit hole of settings that should remain untouched. Gamifying the experience can be another brilliant tactic; create a fun quiz that educates users on the dashboard's purpose while allowing them to explore securely. Finally, implement safeguards against the clicking frenzy with features like confirmation dialogs, which can act as a polite, Are you really sure about that? These can prevent accidental mishaps while ensuring that users don't stumble into a mess of their own making. The idea is to harness their enthusiasm and turn it toward productive exploration rather than wreaking havoc on your carefully constructed dashboards.

13.3 Child-Proofing Your Dashboard: Strategies For User Safety

First, take a moment to picture the chaos that could unfold if your dashboard users were left to their own devices. It's like giving a toddler a pack of crayons and a freshly painted wall—unadulterated mayhem! To equip your dashboards with proper safeguards, you must start by limiting the playground. Role-based access controls are your new best friend. By designating specific permissions based on user roles, you can ensure that only the select few, such as Karen from DevOps (who, let's face it, has earned her stripes), can perform tasks that might result in the digital equivalent of a toddler finger-painting a masterpiece on a server. This means regular users can view and interact with data but won't suddenly find themselves at the helm of the SQL query ship, steering straight towards disaster.

Next, think about implementing error-handling mechanisms, those sneaky little guardians of user experience. When users do something wildly inappropriate—like trying to split an unpluckable chart into three separate pie slices that will never exist—your dashboard should provide a friendly "Oops! That didn't go as planned!" message. Instead of a cold, lifeless error page, give them a laugh. Everyone loves a good joke, especially when it keeps them from accidentally deleting vital data! Consider using input validation to ensure heartwarming moments of spontaneity are kept to a minimum while still leaving room for authentic engagement.

Now let's mosey on over to the art of user-friendliness. Creating a dashboard that feels warm and inviting is like hosting a party where nobody spills punch on the carpet. Dashboard design should consider its audience; big, bold visuals combined with interactive elements can lead to a more engaging user experience. But beware! Excessive information can lead to information overload—a frenzy of data that could send even the most seasoned analyst into a spiral of despair. Striking the right balance is critical. Use color codes and clear labeling that even your least tech-savvy friend would understand. If they can navigate it without a GPS, you're on the right track!

A great way to foster friendly interactions is through helpful tooltips and pop-ups that provide context without smothering the users in text. Rather than saying, "Click here for more," give them a sprightly prompt along the lines of, "Need a hand? Hover over me!" This cheeky interaction encourages exploration while still keeping chaos at bay. When crafting your dashboards, think of it as preparing a meal. The key is to season only to taste: too much salt (or complexity), and you'll send your users running for the nearest sandwich shop (or alternative tool). Keeping it straightforward and intuitive will ensure that your users find delight in their quests to uncover insights rather than peril.

A vital reminder: Always test your dashboard layout with real users—because what works in your mind might just be as confusing as interpreting modern art to someone who thought they were coming to a buffet. User testing can uncover potential pain points you've probably overlooked while slinging pixels around in design mode. Keep it friendly, keep it fun, and remember: a giggle goes a long way in preventing rage-quits!

CHAPTER 14 – GRAFANA CLOUD, ENTERPRISE, OR THE BASEMENT BEAST YOU MAINTAIN ALONE

14.1 Exploring Hosted Options: The Pros And Cons

Hosted Grafana solutions can feel like a breath of fresh air, especially after you've spent weeks wrestling with your own server setup, complete with its own set of rebellious quirks. Just picture it: setting up Grafana on your own machine has all the excitement of assembling IKEA furniture, but with more yelling. Then along comes the star player—hosted Grafana. It promises to take away the headaches while you sip coffee instead of suffering through yet another 'unexpected downtime' saga. No more late-night troubleshooting sessions as you watch your server become the diva of downtime, throwing tantrums like it just lost its favorite toy.

However, let's not forget the dark side of hosted services. The idea of handing over control of your precious data to someone else can feel like playing a high-stakes game of 'Hot Potato.' You get the convenience of letting someone else worry about updates, security patches, and uptime percentages, but there's a nagging worry in the back of your mind: "What happens if they lose it?" Security breaches aren't exactly a rarity in the tech world, and trusting an external service might keep you up at night. That's like letting your neighbor hold your prized fern while you're on vacation, only to find out they thought the fern looked better in the trash.

So, are hosted solutions your golden ticket to IT bliss? Imagine offloading the tedious maintenance and letting someone else deal with the infuriating minutiae of server management. Suddenly, you have extra time to spend on more important things, like figuring out why your coffee machine refuses to turn on after 3 PM, or planning elaborate 'all hands' meetings just to talk about pizza preferences. A hosted Grafana service gives you that freedom to focus on creating meaningful dashboards instead of staring at logs until your screen starts looking like a Jackson Pollock painting made of error messages.

The conclusion of this IT carnival is that hosted services can provide an enticing solution to those who are willing to relinquish some control. Weigh the benefits and drawbacks carefully because, at the end of the day, your data deserves a loving home, whether it's in the hands of a cloud service or your own carefully crafted basement beast that you lovingly maintain alone. A practical tip? Before you commit, consider spinning up a trial version of a hosted Grafana service. Nothing like a little taste test before you dive into the buffet of cloud offerings!

14.2 The Joy Of Offloading Responsibility: Grafana Cloud Benefits

Embracing Grafana Cloud is like opening a big box of stress-free magic. Imagine, no more waking up at 3 a.m. to the sound of your server burping error messages as it struggles under the weight of your ambitious dashboard. Instead, Grafana Cloud lifts that load right off your shoulders, letting you dedicate more time to the important things in life, like perfecting your coffee-making skills or contemplating the deeper meaning of life—while wearing pajamas, of course. Think about it: gone are the days of fidgeting nervously while performing complex rubber band calculations on your server's performance. With Grafana Cloud, your workload transforms into a delightful cloud of rainbows and sunshine, where someone else handles the nitty-gritty. What's better? You still get to pop into your dashboard and flex those analytical muscles without the hassle of managing infrastructure.

Letting somebody else juggle the intricate responsibility of maintenance is like delegating your daily broccoli to a friend who actually enjoys eating it. Imagine all that glorious free time! You can now enjoy the thrill of dashboard creation without frequency-induced heart palpitations. What's that? Your service is down? Not anymore. With Grafana Cloud, you can confidently throw around industry jargon like "metric redundancy" while sipping on your smoothie, knowing that professionals are behind the curtain waving their wands to keep everything running smoothly. You can turn your attention to the real joys in life, such as testing every plugin available on the Grafana marketplace just to see how far it bends reality—if you dare. This freedom allows for creativity to flourish without the constraints of server updates and patch management. So go ahead, play the part of the mad scientist—just this time, the lab is clean, and you don't have to wash the beakers!

14.3 Maintaining Your Own Grafana: Tales Of The Basement Beast

Maintaining your own Grafana instance is a bit like living with an eccentric roommate who has a flair for dramatics. One minute, you're soaring high on the exhilarating rush of monitoring all the metrics you could ever want, and the next, you're knee-deep in the chaos brought on by your beloved "basement beast"—that old server you lovingly named Carl. This creature often demands your attention at the most inconvenient of times. You might find yourself frantically Googling how to troubleshoot Grafana when a simple coffee spill leads Carl to an unexpected crash, leaving you to ponder if the universe is conspiring against your monitoring setup.

The quirks of maintaining Grafana are endless. One day, the data synchronizes perfectly, presenting you with dashboards that make you feel like a dashboard wizard. The next day, it's an unpredictable mess, filled with wild fluctuations in data, missing queries, and a dashboard that looks like it has been put together by a cat walking across the keyboard. Debugging in this chaotic environment can make you wonder whether Carl secretly has a vendetta against your sanity. It takes both patience and humor to deal with the whims of this "basement beast" and to ensure that it continues to show you the data you desperately need—while also resisting the urge to toss a few cups at the wall during moments of exasperation.

To keep your passion project alive amidst the chaos, it's essential to embrace the unpredictable nature of your setup. Just like a quirky sitcom, each day will bring new surprises that keep you on your toes. Establishing a solid routine can help manage the chaos. Regular updates on Grafana and consistent monitoring will save you headaches over time, and thinking of your patches and tweaks like a weekly health check on your best friend Carl can remind you that keeping your system happy requires a personal touch. Set aside time each week for routine maintenance. Having a set schedule means you can address potential hiccups before they escalate into full-blown disasters. Keep a cozy, chaotic corner in your attic or basement dedicated to Grafana diagnostics— loaded with coffee, snacks, and maybe a stress ball or two—so you can dive into troubleshooting with a motivated spirit.

Engaging with the Grafana community can also breathe new life into your project. Forums and user groups abound with fellow enthusiasts who have faced similar trials. Sharing your own tales of the basement beast can be cathartic, and exchanging tips about plugins or plugins gone rogue can give you those lightning flashes of inspiration that help you refine your graphs. Remember, every time you conquer a metric, you're not just enhancing your monitoring; you're adding to your own mythology of the basement beast. In every affront from Carl, there lies an opportunity for wisdom—like the time a random SQL query became the magic spell that made everything click perfectly. Hold onto those wins, speak of them often, and relish in the calamity of maintaining your own Grafana.

CHAPTER 15 – ZEN AND THE ART OF DASHBOARD MAINTENANCE

15.1 The Quest For Alignment: Tips For Panel Perfection

Picture this: your dashboard is a stunning masterpiece of data visualization, but here comes the panel alignment drama! It's as if each panel has a personality crisis and decides it's time to do the cha-cha while you're expecting a solemn ballet of data. Fear not! With a few tips, you can turn that chaotic dance floor into a synchronized swim team. First, always remember to check your grid settings; if your panels think they're competing in a 'who can be the most awkwardly placed' contest, a little grid adjustment will bring them to heel. Experiment with padding and margins, making sure your panels feel comfortable but not too spacious —nobody likes awkward breathing room in a dance-off, after all. And don't forget to apply the magical 'Align Left' or 'Center' buttons like a trusted spell; they can work wonders in restoring order to the chaos.

When things get unruly, break the tension with humor—after all, what's a missing pixel between friends? Embrace the art of patience; align each panel like an artist carefully placing each stroke. Use the 'Preview' mode in Grafana rather than shaking your fist in anger at that stubborn panel; it could be your best friend for avoiding catastrophic alignment failures. And hey, keyboard shortcuts can become your secret weapon! Master those shortcuts to toggle through settings faster than a squirrel at a nut festival. Just don't let one tiny alignment mistake ruin your day —take a deep breath, tap into your inner Zen, and realign with the grace of a dance instructor correcting a stray ballet dancer. Remember, dashboards can be part of a comedy show, so let them bring you joy even in the face of misalignments!

15.2 Documentation: The Unsung Hero Of Dashboard Zen

Documentation is that unassuming hero in the superhero film of data management. While dashboards spark joy and create visual kabooms of information, it's the documentation that ensures every incoming storm of queries, updates, and changes can be weathered without capsizing the ship. Imagine trying to maintain a dashboard without a GPS—one quirk in the software, and you're adrift in a sea of confusion. Clear, precise documentation acts like a map etched in the stars, guiding weary developers and frantic database administrators back to the shores of sanity. You might think, But who needs documentation when I have a memory like an elephant? Well, even elephants forget birthdays—and when that birthday bash involves legacy code or a rogue plugin from the Dark Ages of 2020, it's nice to have reminders detailing your past decisions to guide you. The clarity that documentation brings allows onboarding new team members to not feel like a scavenger hunt and lets you prevent yelling at your monitor as you remember you once had a great solution to an annoying problem but can't recall where you saved it.

Documentation doesn't have to be an eternal slog through the dark, dreary tunnel of monotony. Turn it into an adventure worthy of a quest in a fantasy novel! Think of your documentation as a magical spell book, filled with potions and incantations that can pull any fellow coder from the dark depths of confusion. Inject some pizzazz into your documentation. Instead of This function calculates total sales, try This magnificent function weaves together the magical threads of data to conjure the total sales, bringing forth a bounty of numbers that sing with profitability! You can even add doodles, memes, or gifs that express the complicated emotions you feel during integration. Collaborate with teammates to create "documentation day" marathons, complete with snacks and a competitive spirit—who can write the best (or weirdest) description of that pesky data pipeline? By transforming documentation into a creative outlet, it evolves from a chore into a team-building exercise filled with laughter, engagement, and perhaps a cheeky meme or two. The more enjoyable the process, the more likely you and your team will keep those docs updated, ensuring that future navigators won't find themselves lost in the world of analytics.

15.3 Finding Peace In The Dashboard Chaos

Finding peace in the chaos of dashboard maintenance is like looking for a needle in a haystack, except the needle is a well-aligned pie chart, and the haystack is made of incorrectly configured data sources. The journey begins with breathing exercises—yes, you heard it right. A deep inhalation as you confront your nearest data visualization that looks more like abstract art than a representation of actual data can work wonders. Embrace the absurdity of that moment, chuckle softly as you wonder who in the world thought a donut chart represented your server downtime, and then get to work with a zen mindset. Take a page from the meditation world's book and practice gratitude. Be thankful first for each dashboard you maintain, no matter how clunky they may be, because they've allowed you to glimpse into patterns of users, traffic, and other oddities that can save the world—or at least your project. With every chaotic poke and prod at the data, remind yourself that there is a method buried beneath that mountain of metadata.

Mindfulness can be a game-changer in dashboard maintenance. Picture this: instead of frantically clicking every button like a hungry raccoon rummaging through a trash can, you pause. You breathe. You sip your coffee because it's a scientifically proven fear-fighting mechanism. Watch your dashboard with the same scrutiny you'd give a toddler working on a finger painting. Each pixel out of place and every sluggish refresh becomes a small opportunity for improvement rather than a source of chaos. Implementing a routine is critical. Schedule your dashboard checks with the seriousness one might reserve for a dentist appointment. It's true; a monthly mindfulness session with your dashboards can bring clarity. Dive deep into the analytics without distractions—turn your phone to silent and seal off the world while you unlock the secrets of line graphs and the wisdom hidden in their slopes. In doing so, you transform your chaotic dashboard interactions into a tranquil experience of data discovery, allowing for a newly cultivated appreciation of pie charts that don't make your head spin.

Remember that understanding the data flow requires a patient, playful approach. Treating the dashboard like an unrollable burrito wrap—full of surprises, maybe a bit messy but completely edible—invites creativity. Whenever you feel the chaos overwhelming, take a step back and practice a mindfulness hack: visualize your alerts as gentle reminders rather than terrifying sirens heralding doom. After all, those alerts—whether a simple email or a bombastic Slack notification—are just the dashboard's way of saying, "Hey buddy, you might want to look at this."

APPENDIX A: THE GRAFANA CLI COOKBOOK

A.1 Essential Commands and Tips

It's time to arm yourself with the essential Grafana CLI commands that every admin should know, like a culinary wizard with a spatula of infinite power. Whether you're wrangling with graph visuals or patching up disaster scenarios, these commands are your secret arsenal. First, let's talk about some basics. The first command you should memorize is grafana-cli admin reset-admin-password. Imagine it saving you from an embarrassing call to IT when you forget that supposedly easy-to-remember password. Next up, grafana-cli plugins list will reveal all the ways you've expanded Grafana's abilities. It's like going through your childhood toy box, only to find that remote-controlled dinosaur you forgot you had. Then there's grafana-cli plugins install, an intergalactic sounding command that allows you to install new plugins faster than the speed of light—well, figuratively speaking.

Now that you have a few commands in your hip pocket, let's get tipsy... um, I mean, let's dive into some tips for using those commands effectively and effortlessly. You want to be like a graceful gazelle, bounding across the savannah of commands without looking like you tripped over your own feet. Keep your command-line interface (CLI) clean and organized. Comment your scripts using # to remind future you what on Earth you were thinking. And remember, practice makes perfect; use --help often for any command you don't fully trust. This will be your best friend when you're lost in the woods of flags and arguments. If all else fails, remember that Google and community forums are your backup singers, ready to harmonize in perfect pitch when your brain hits a high note of confusion. The ultimate tip? When in doubt, try not to execute commands that sound dangerous, like grafana-cli admin reset... except for when you really need to.

A.2 Common CLI Tasks for Dashboard Management

Working with dashboards can feel like a delightful carnival ride or an impenetrable maze, depending on how familiar you are with the command line interface (CLI). For dashboard management, a sprinkle of CLI magic can transform a tedious task into a walk in the park—albeit a park filled with friendly squirrels and a few confused raccoons. Simple tasks like checking the status of your dashboard, adding data sources, or updating your plugins can be achieved swiftly with just a handful of commands. The secret sauce? Knowing where to type!

First off, let's tackle the almighty command to check your dashboard's health. You can type "grafana-cli admin check-admin" to ensure everything's running as smooth as butter on a hot day. If the response includes a "Yes, you are the boss!" it's time to do a little happy dance and proceed to the next task. Want to get those data sources added without jumping through web interface hoops? A swift "grafana-cli data add" followed by your data source configuration will save you time and bewilderment during your next meeting. The CLI is not just a set of commands; it's like having a personal assistant who knows exactly what you want without the need for awkward small talk!

Everybody's hunting for shortcuts in the world of dashboards, and let's be honest, who wouldn't want to turn drudgery into smooth sailing? Why click through endless menus when you can input a magical command and watch everything come together like a well-rehearsed flash mob? Enter the wonder that is scripting! By automating repetitive tasks with little shell scripts, you can make the CLI your best friend—the kind that shows up with coffee and cake every Monday morning.

Imagine this: instead of opening Grafana and frantically rearranging panels, you can write a script to deploy those settings like you own the place. Just type "bash deploy_dashboard.sh" and voilà, your dashboard is set up just how you like it! Remember to add that little note in the comments section of your script; a dash of humor doesn't hurt, especially when you're elbow-deep in queries. Plus, you'll be the dashboard rock star everyone admires for your dazzling efficiency and quirky quips. Make these CLI tasks your playbook, and you'll save time, sanity, and perhaps even the occasional unnecessary team meeting. Who knows, maybe you'll become the office luminary known for rapid dashboard enhancements and wit as sharp as a tack!

A.3 Troubleshooting CLI Issues Like a Pro

Imagine you're in a high-stakes game of whack-a-mole with your command line. Each time you think you've squashed that pesky error, another one pops up, mocking you from the screen like a cat that just knocked over a glass of water. The key to troubleshooting CLI issues is to channel your inner Zen master, or in this case, Zen programmer. Approach each error message as if it were a riddle waiting to be solved, not a malevolent force trying to suck your will to live. Start by reading the error message slowly, letting each word wash over you like the soothing sounds of whale music. What does it say? Is there a specific command mentioned? Did you just forget to add that oh-so-essential `sudo`?

Next, gather your debugging tools. Much like a chef wouldn't slay a boar with a butter knife, you need the right utilities to tackle your CLI conundrums. Tools like `grep`, `awk`, and `sed` can become your trusty companions. They're like the Swiss Army knives in your digital toolbox, ready to slice through verbosity and help you get straight to the heart of the problem. For example, if a script isn't running as expected, use `tail -f` to watch logs in real time, treating the log files like your favorite drama series —full of suspense and plot twists. As you hone your skills, you'll start to see patterns in the chaos, making you feel like the Sherlock Holmes of the terminal.

Once you've dived into the depths of your CLI issues, it's time to turn that frown upside down. Transforming troubleshooting trials into triumphant victories requires a sprinkle of creativity and a lot of patience. When you finally decipher that enigmatic error code like it's an ancient scroll revealing the secrets of the universe, take a moment to savor the sweet taste of victory. Celebrate small wins, whether it's getting your script to run successfully or finally understanding what the `404 Not Found` error really means. Each little triumph adds another trophy to your collection, even if it's just a new stickie note proclaiming I fixed it!

Don't shy away from sharing your newfound knowledge. Pass it on to your fellow developers or project managers. Settle into your comfortable chair, make a pot of coffee, and prepare for the awed expressions of your audience as you regale them with tales of your triumphs over the CLI—a true gladiator in the arena of ones and zeros. Use social media or internal forums to share your CLI conquests and the eye-opening revelations that came with them. Not only does this foster a thriving community, but you might just inspire someone else to tackle their own CLI challenges. With every error you conquer, remember that you're not just fixing problems; you're becoming an unstoppable force of technical wizardry!

As a practical tip, always keep a notebook or digital document handy to jot down common CLI errors and their solutions. This can save you time and sanity down the line, creating a personalized manual that's uniquely yours, or perhaps, a quirky memoir of your tech adventures.

APPENDIX B: 101 EXCUSES FOR WHEN ALERTS GO OFF AT 3AM

B.1 The Best (and Worst) Excuses to Tell Your Boss

When the sun is still snoozing and your phone decides to erupt into a cacophony of alerts, a genius excuse can make all the difference. Imagine stumbling into the office bleary-eyed and disheveled, only to flash a grin and say, "Oh, I just got lost in the Bermuda Triangle of our server logs. You know how it is!" This sends a message that you're both in control and a little quirky, which can be charming. If you prefer a whimsical flair, claiming you were up negotiating a peace treaty between our servers and the toaster, which has been consuming bandwidth like a hungry hippo, might just earn you a chuckle or two.

There's always the reliable "I was rescuing a drowning VPN." The image of a heroic you, diving headfirst into the digital depths of connectivity issues can turn a horrifying wake-up call into a glorious tale. You could also channel your inner sleeper agent: "I was on a deep cover mission to identify our network's villain. Spoiler: it's definitely not the coffee machine." With the right blend of humor and creativity, you can spin those night-time alerts into entertaining anecdotes, ensuring your colleagues and boss see you as a reliable problem-solver rather than just the person glued to Slack at unholy hours.

If humor is your secret weapon, you can confidently dodge any awkwardness after a night of unexpected alerts. Picture this: when asked why an alert went off at such an ungodly hour, you can say, "I thought it was a notification from the 'Snooze Your Responsibilities' app. Turns out it was our database throwing a late-night tantrum." It lightens the mood while subtly indicating your presence of mind. Or try, "I was conducting a thrilling interrogation of our server. The answers were unsatisfactory, hence the alerts!" This not only hints at your investigative prowess but also shows your ability to turn glaring issues into engaging storytelling.

Another fun tactic is to reference pop culture. "Honestly, I thought I was just saving Gotham, but it turns out our monitoring tools had a mind of their own!" Making light of a stressful situation can create a stronger bond with your team, while still keeping you in the clear professionally. People appreciate a good laugh, especially when they relate it to their struggles. Add some flair with, "Next time I'm installing a sleep mode on our monitoring system," to show that not only do you recognize the chaos, you're thinking of creative solutions. Remember, a little laugh goes a long way in nurturing a professional persona that can tackle anything, even at 3 AM!

B.2 Avoiding the 'Oops' Moment: How to Prepare

Preventing those cringe-inducing 'oops' moments begins with thorough preparation. First, it pays to know your alerts as if they were the offspring of your most devoted plant; tender, caring, and a wee bit neurotic. Spend some time familiarizing yourself with the alert conditions that truly require your immediate attention.

If you set alerts for every little hiccup, you'll find yourself swimming in a tsunami of notifications, making it feel like the universe is in constant chaos. Instead, choose wisely, establishing thresholds for what really indicates that the sky is falling, or rather, when Bob has mistakenly thought the toaster was an IT switch.

Consider creating a foolproof checklist before you dive into the exciting world of monitoring. Think beyond the basics: does your alert system still make sense? Is it still sane after the inevitable software updates? Included in this should also be a script to remind everyone of the 'do not panic' protocol, perhaps affixed to the fridge in the break room for easy reference. Each step in your preparation should be like a yoga class for your mind, stretching your capacity for chaos, aligning your processes with clarity, and maybe even throwing in a downward dog or two to breathe before alerts start going off like confetti at a surprise party.

There's no joy in waking up at 3 AM to alerts popping off like surprise popcorn kernels in a room full of light sleepers. To avoid this, streamline your alerting system and implement some friendly time windows where alerts can take a vacation. For example, set business hours for your alerts, so they don't intrude while you're dreaming about pizza or defending the noble cause of dashboard optimization. When the clock strikes midnight, let your systems rest, nestled in the warmth of code instead of alert ruckus.

It may also be wise to implement a dual-layered alert strategy. First, focus on high-severity incidents that might signal impending doom or meltdowns, and separate them from regular noise like a toddler knocking over a stack of blocks. Send critical alerts to a dedicated channel with its own rules and perhaps a celebratory GIF or two for those who can skillfully handle chaos. Encourage your team to embrace tech like parents embracing the spills and thrills of parenting — one step at a time and with a dab of humor. You'll reduce the midnight panic and transform those 'oops' moments into opportunities for growth, resulting in a smoother-sailing team where alerts won't puncture the serenity of your sleep without a good reason.

For those late-night tech warriors who still find themselves panicking, consider designing alerts with a touch of whimsy. Sound effects or quirky message tones can add just the right amount of levity to the onslaught of information, letting your team know that chaos may be calling, but it can currently wait for breakfast.

B.3 Turning Chaos into Humor: Making Light of Late Night Alerts

Late-night alerts are like surprise parties you never wanted, where the guest of honor is a critical failure and the cake is stale stress. There's nothing quite like the jolt of adrenaline that comes at 2 AM when your phone lights up with an alert that your server is, quite certifiably, on fire. It feels like your heart just skipped three beats, and you momentarily question every life choice you've made. But rather than letting that panic seep into your veins, why not embrace the chaos with some humor? Think of those moments—when the alert pops up saying Database Down!—as the beginning of a zany tale. You can envision yourself as the unwitting protagonist of a horror-comedy, navigating the absurdity of late-night tech troubles. Each alert can become fodder for rich anecdotes that not only lighten the turmoil but make for hilarious retellings at the next team meeting.

Transforming those stress-laden nights into comedy gold can involve a little imagination and a healthy dose of sarcasm. Did you ever find yourself frantically looking through logs as if they were ancient scrolls containing the secrets of the universe? The moment you realize the critical issue was just Bob's coffee cup spilling on the server is a gem that will draw a laugh. By sharing these experiences, you create an atmosphere where everyone can relate to the absurdity of tech life, preparing better for future chaos while seeing the humor in the madness. So, grab those late-night alerts and twist them into funny tales that keep the work environment lighthearted, turning your midnight fiascoes into comedies worth a standing ovation.

Managing alerts doesn't have to be a frantic race against the clock fueled by Red Bull and panic. In fact, tackling chaos with humor offers a surprisingly effective antidote to the anxiety that often accompanies those late-night wake-up calls. Instead of hiding from the fear of what an alert might signify, embrace it as an opportunity for laughter. Picture yourself in the midst of what feels like a high-stakes mission, only to realize that your greatest foe is, of all things, an unrebooted router. Whenever possible, infuse action plans with light humor. For instance, when communicating with your team about what went wrong, consider preemptively quipping, "So, who wants to bet Bob's up next to unplug something again?" Each of these small moments of levity can act as stress relievers and bond-builders within your team.

Using humor also encourages open conversations about operational mishaps. When you're comfortable laughing at errors or unexpected alerts, it creates an environment where others feel at ease to share their blunders without fear of judgment. You can swap stories over coffee, recounting the time the database theft alert turned out to be nothing more than a misconfigured permission setting. That ability to laugh together not only mitigates the horror of the alerts but reinforces a collective resilience against whatever tech monsters the night shifts may bring. The next time the phone lights up like a disco ball at a debugging dance-off, remember: a light-hearted approach doesn't just diffuse tension; it also strengthens camaraderie, paving the way for a team that can handle the wildest alerts with a smile.

APPENDIX C: DASHBOARD HAIKU AND ASCII ART

C.1 Crafting Dashboard Haikus: A Creative Outlet

Writing haikus inspired by your dashboard data is a delightful way to blend creativity with numbers. Crafting these charming three-line poems urges you to find the poetic essence in the metrics that often seem like mere rows and columns. Imagine translating that labyrinth of CPU usage, memory consumption, and user interactions into delicate verses. Instead of just crunching numbers, you can paint a picture with your data. Picture your CPU usage graph: thumbnail a serene line of harmony as you explore high usage in a haiku. "Data points ascend, CPU climbs like mountain peaks, numbers sing their song." By engaging in this playful exercise, you awaken the hidden rhythms within your statistics.

This process not only lightens the mood surrounding your analytics but turns a tedious task into a zany creative workshop. It's the perfect excuse to step away from spreadsheets and find joy amidst those incessant Slack alerts. You'll find yourself giggling over the absurdity of your data, writing verses about that one dashboard that just won't cooperate. Instead of cursing at the error logs, why not wax poetic? "Empty pie displays a hunger, pixels yearn to be filled, graphs weeping for life." This approach fosters a cheerful interaction with the numbers you might have previously ignored, transforming frustration into inspiration—who knew logs could harbor such creative potential! When you allow the art of haiku to dance with your dashboard, you enrich your work life and spark a newfound love for the data you chase every day.

Diving into this zany practice can unleash unexpected joy. It serves as a reminder that even the most mundane numbers harbor stories waiting to be told. So grab a cup of coffee (or something stronger if that's your preferred fuel), your favorite dashboard, and start to play. Challenge yourself to capture the essence of a particularly perplexing data point in seventeen syllables or less. Your co-workers might raise their eyebrows at first, but once they see your spirited interpretations, they might just join in on the fun. Don't be surprised if you find that your haikus become the unexpected highlight of your team meetings, giving everyone a chuckle even amidst the chaos of server alerts. And who knows? You might just inspire a new movement: the art of dashboard haikus!

C.2 The Art of ASCII: Expressing Data Like a 90s Prodigy

ASCII art is the unsung hero of digital nostalgia, a true relic from the glorious days of tech when monochrome screens roamed the Earth, and dot-matrix printers had us living life on the edge with every page print. This art form transforms plain old data into whimsical representations that can stir memories of long-gone dial-up tones and pixelated graphics. Whether you're looking to create charming pie charts crafted from character ciphers or dignified line graphs made from dashes, ASCII lets you strut your retro stuff while maintaining a professional edge. Remember, before the advent of flashy GUI elements, programmers used their imaginations to visualize data through meticulous placements of letters and symbols, proving that even the most humble of characters can hold a wealth of visual information.

Integrating ASCII designs into your dashboards isn't just about adding a sprinkle of fun; it's about capturing the hearts of fellow code warriors who appreciate the mastery of making data appear not only functional but fantastically entertaining. Picture a dashboard wherein every metric is flanked by tiny aliens dancing in delight as SQL queries deliver sweet, sweet data. Or, envision your uptime metrics displayed through a delightful ASCII tower, dramatically collapsing as outages occur. Such zany visuals can lighten the mood during the data drag while proving that dashboards don't have to suck the life out of users. By mastering this retro art, you can transform numbers and graphs into compelling narratives, inviting curiosity and reducing anxiety often associated with data overload.

Imagine your standard dashboard metamorphosing into a digital canvas where data doesn't just flow, it dances! With a sprinkle of ASCII art, your metrics can tell stories with flair—each line and letter layering onto the next to create a visual feast. Picture a glorious traffic light made entirely of keyboard characters signaling uptime, with each very functional color block flashing its significance. It's not merely about repurposing tables and panels; it's about elevating data from a mere presentation to an exhibition that captivates the hearts and minds of viewers, leaving a lingering smile that says, I love data, and I also value fun!

For an extra touch of whimsicality, consider using ASCII as a visual aid for alerts. Instead of the usual alarm bells, imagine receiving a leisurely stroll-through animated GIF of ASCII artwork illustrating the impending doom of your CPU maxing out. Such creativity can soften the blow of bad news, making it easier to address potential disasters with laughter instead of panic. So, as you concoct your next dashboard, remember to let your imagination soar; maybe throw in a well-placed ASCII cat for good measure—it might just be the most productive thing you do all day.

C.3 Blending Humor and Data: A Final Creative Touch

Embracing the creativity of blending humor into data presentations can transform a mundane report into a delightful experience that sparks interest. Picture this: instead of presenting a serious pie chart about quarterly sales, you throw in a cartoon of a pie-eating contest where the winner gets a trophy of... a pie! This lighthearted approach makes the data stick, turning "Oh look, sales are down" into "Yikes, looks like our sales pie has more slices missing than my fridge during finals week!" It's all about using clever visuals, witty commentary, and relatable analogies to take the chill out of what can often be dry statistics.

Final thoughts on keeping our data narratives enjoyable and compelling revolve around the idea that data doesn't have to be a snooze fest. Use playful anecdotes or zany comparisons that invite chuckles while still conveying the necessary information. Perhaps when illustrating a spike in server usage, you liken it to your teen's sudden demand for Wi-Fi when their favorite show drops a new season. By creating a narrative that feels engaging and connected to the real world, you humanize your data, allowing others to grasp the significance without dozing off. So, keep those data stories spicy, relatable, and above all, fun. Remember, the goal is for your audience to leave with a smile—and that nugget of information that will haunt their thoughts long after the dashboard session ends.